Collins · *do brilliantly!*

Exam**Practice**

ASPsychology

Exam practice at its **best**

■ **Mike Cardwell**

■ **Claire Meldrum**

■ **Jane Willson**

■ **Series Editor: Jayne de Courcy**

Contents

William Collins' dream of knowledge for all began with the publication of his first book in 1819. A self-educated mill worker, he not only enriched millions of lives, but also founded a flourishing publishing house. Today, staying true to this spirit, Collins books are packed with inspiration, innovation and practical expertise. They place you at the centre of a world of possibility and give you exactly what you need to explore it.

Collins. Do more.

Published by Collins
An imprint of HarperCollins*Publishers*
77–85 Fulham Palace Road
Hammersmith
London
W6 8JB

Browse the complete Collins catalogue at
www.collinseducation.com

© HarperCollins*Publishers* Ltd 2006

First published 2001
This revised edition published 2006

10 9 8 7 6 5 4 3 2 1

ISBN-13 978 0 00 721549 2
ISBN-10 0 00 721549 5

Mike Cardwell, Claire Meldrum and Jane Willson assert their moral right to be identified as the authors of this work.

British Library Cataloguing in Publication Data
A catalogue record for this book is available from the British Library

Acknowledgements

Illustrations
Cartoon Artwork – Roger Penwill
DTP Artwork – Geoff Ward

Photographs
The Authors and Publisher are grateful to the following for permission to reproduce photographs:
© Bettmann/CORBIS 53; © Howard Davies/CORBIS 64; Sheena Verdun Taylor 21, 31, 42, 77

Every effort has been made to contact the holders of copyright material, but if any have been inadvertently overlooked, the Publishers will be pleased to make the necessary arrangements at the first opportunity.

Edited by Brigitte Lee and Sue Chapple
Picture research by Ginny Stroud-Lewis
Production by Katie Butler
Book design by Bob Vickers and Gecko Limited
Printed and bound by Printing Express, Hong Kong

You might also like to visit:
www.harpercollins.com
The book lover's website

How this book will help you

by Mike Cardwell, Claire Meldrum and Jane Willson

This book will help you to improve your performance in the AQA (Specification A) AS level Psychology exam. **This specification for Psychology has six topics, organized into three modules**. Each topic is split into 'subsections'. For example, 'Stress' is divided into 'Stress as a bodily response' and 'Sources of stress'. Each of these topics (except for 'Research Methods') is also accompanied by a '**critical issue**', which covers an aspect of the topic that is an important application of that topic. For example, an application of 'Human memory' is 'Eye-witness testimony'.

The topics covered by your AQA–A specification

The AQA–A topics, subsections and critical issues (plus appropriate chapters in this book) are as follows:

Topic	Critical Issue	*Exam Practice* Chapter number
MODULE 1		
Human memory ● Short-term and long-term memory ● Forgetting	Eye-witness testimony	1
Attachments in development ● The development and variety of attachments ● Deprivation and privation	Day care	2
MODULE 2		
Stress ● Stress as a bodily response ● Sources of stress	Stress management	3
Abnormality ● Defining psychological abnormality ● Biological and psychological models of abnormality	Eating disorders	4
MODULE 3		
Social influence ● Conformity and minority influence ● Obedience to authority	Ethical issues	5
Research methods ● Qualitative and quantitative research methods ● Research design and implementation ● Data analysis	–	6

Students frequently fail to perform as well as they might in exams because they have poor **exam skills** or cannot apply what they know effectively. This is evident from how surprised many students are when they receive an exam grade that bears little relation to the amount of work they have done in preparation for the exam.

To get a good grade in AS level Psychology you need a good grasp of the subject matter and good exam technique. Your main textbook will help you to develop your knowledge and understanding. **This book can help you improve your exam technique, so that you can make the most effective use of what you know**.

Each of the six chapters in this book (relating to the six sections of the AQA–A AS level Psychology specification) is broken down into five separate elements. Each chapter has the following sections:

❶ Exam Questions and 'Choosing the best question'

Each chapter starts with two typical exam questions of the sort you will find on a real AQA–A AS level Psychology paper. In your exam (except for the Research Methods questions), you will only be expected to answer one of these two questions. The **'Choosing the best question'** section shows you what to look for when reading through the questions and helps you **select the question that is likely to yield most marks for you**.

❷ Students' Answers and 'How to score full marks'

For one of the exam questions we provide two **typical students' answers**. These answers show many of the **most common mistakes** that students make under exam conditions, but also how well-prepared students can deal effectively with the time constraints of an exam question.

The students' answers are followed by a section called **'How to score full marks'**. This shows you where and how the answers could be improved, e.g. we explain exactly what the question is asking for; we point out missing knowledge; we show you how you can best deal with the AO2 requirement of the question. **This means that when you meet these sorts of question in your exam, you will know how to tackle them effectively in order to score high marks**.

For the last part of the questions (which is worth more marks) we also provide an **additional short commentary** alongside the students' answers, pointing out what is good, not so good and what is missing.

❸ 'Don't forget...' boxes

These boxes highlight some of the most important things to remember when answering questions on a particular topic. They also highlight some of the common mistakes that students make when answering exam questions in that area. When you're doing your last-minute revision you can quickly read through these boxes in all six chapters and make doubly sure you are ready to answer questions without making any easily avoidable mistakes.

❹ 'Key points to remember'

The 'Key points to remember' section of each chapter gives you a quick overview of the topic as a whole and presents the most important points that you will need to cover when revising that topic. Remember, however, that a book of this size can't hope to cover all the detailed psychological information that you need for your exam – that's what your textbook, class notes and assignments are for! Make sure you use these alongside this book.

❺ Question to try, Answers and Examiner's comments

Each chapter ends with an exam question for you to try answering. The best way to do this is to try to answer it as if you were in an exam. Try to remember all that you've read earlier in the chapter and put it into practice here. It is particularly important to keep to the same times for each question that you would be allowed in the proper exam. It is best to find out now just what the time pressures are going to be like in your exam.

When you've written your answer, check it through and turn to the back of the book. There you'll find an answer to the question that you've just done. The answer is of a very good 'A' grade standard. We've added our 'Examiner's comments' on it to show you exactly why it's such a good answer.

Compare your answer with the answer given. If you feel yours isn't as good, you can use the one given and our comments on it to help you decide which aspects of your answer you could improve on. You may find, for example, that you can incorporate sections of the answer given into your own answer, and you can use our comments to judge whether your own answer has covered the key issues. Remember, though, that there is no such thing as a 'perfect answer'. If your answer and the 'model' answer differ merely in content, then yours may be every bit as good as the one given here, and would warrant just as many marks.

What is in the exam?

In the AQA–A exam, you will sit three exam papers or 'units'. Each of these corresponds to the material from a 'module'. You have to study all the material in these modules, although there will be a choice of questions in the exam. All of the three 'subsections' in each area (e.g. 'Stress as a bodily response', 'Sources of stress' and 'Stress management') will be represented across the two questions from which you make your choice. This doesn't mean that all three will be in each question, but it does mean that you can't afford to be selective in your revision. The advice given in the '**Choosing the best question**' part of each chapter will help you make the right decision when choosing which of the two questions to answer. There is only one question in the Research Methods section, and this is compulsory.

AO1, AO2 and AO3

AQA–A AS level questions assess **three types of skill**. These skills, known as 'Assessment Objectives', are as follows:

Knowledge and Understanding (AO1)

Analysis and Evaluation (AO2)

Designing, Conducting and Reporting (AO3)

AO3 questions are restricted to the Research Methods section, but AO1 and AO2 questions are present in all the other topics. Each question is worth 30 marks, with the AO1 parts of the question being worth 18 marks and the AO2 component of each question being worth 12 marks.

The first two parts of each question (except for Research Methods) are always AO1 and the last part always AO1 **plus** AO2. This is important because different types of questions require different types of answer. AO1 questions require more **descriptive responses** whereas AO1 + AO2 questions require more **evaluative responses**.

Examples of the types of questions

The following are examples of the types of questions that are used to assess AO1 and AO2. (This book contains many more such examples.) Remember that each mark is equivalent to approximately **one minute** of thinking and writing, so it is vital to use this time wisely, neither extending it nor skimping on it.

AO1 questions

What is meant by the terms conformity, minority influence, and obedience?

[2 + 2 + 2 marks]

Describe two differences between short-term (STM) and long-term (LTM) memory.

[3 + 3 marks]

Describe the aims/procedures/findings/conclusions* of one study of reconstructive memory. [* any combination of two aspects of this study]   [6 marks]

Describe the procedures and findings of one study of conformity.   [6 marks]

Outline findings of research into the effects of day care on children's social development.

[6 marks]

Outline one explanation of attachment (e.g. Bowlby).   [6 marks]

Outline two explanations of forgetting in long-term memory.   [3 + 3 marks]

Give two criticisms of the general adaptation syndrome.   [3 + 3 marks]

AO2 questions

To what extent has psychological research shown eyewitness testimony to be unreliable?

[18 marks]

Give a brief account of, and evaluate the use of ethical guidelines as a way of resolving ethical issues in psychological research.   [18 marks]

'An individual's personality type may well be one of the most important influences in how they are affected by stress.'

Consider the role played by personality in modifying the effects of stressors.

[18 marks]

The following tables give an insight into how the marks are awarded for the most common of the AQA–A question types used in the AS level Psychology exam. These are **summaries** of the marking allocation tables used by examiners, but **they contain the same mark divisions and criteria**.

In the **AO1** questions, the emphasis is on the **amount of relevant material presented** (e.g. 'limited' or 'basic'), **the amount of detail given** (e.g. 'lacking detail') and **the accuracy of the material** (e.g. 'muddled').

In the AO1 + AO2 part of the question, the emphasis is not only on the descriptive content (AO1), but also on the **amount and level** of the critical commentary (e.g. 'superficial'), its **thoroughness** (e.g. 'reasonably thorough') and **how effectively it has been used** (e.g. 'highly effective'). This is the AO2 component of the question, and in the final part of each question this is worth 12 of the 18 marks available.

AO1 2-mark questions

For example:

> What is meant by the terms conformity, minority influence and obedience? [2 + 2 + 2 marks]

2 marks Accurate and detailed
1 mark Basic, lacking detail, muddled or flawed
0 marks Inappropriate or incorrect

AO1 3- and 6-mark questions

For example:

> Outline two explanations of forgetting in short-term memory. [3 + 3 marks]
>
> Outline findings of research into the effects of day care on children's social development. [6 marks]

3-mark questions	6-mark questions	Criteria
3	6-5	Accurate and detailed
2	4-3	Limited, generally accurate but less detailed
1	2-1	Basic, lacking in detail, muddled or flawed
0	0	Inaccurate or irrelevant

AO1 + AO2 questions

As all AO1 + AO2 questions are worth 18 marks (6 marks for AO1 and 12 for AO2), the following table applies to **the AO2 component in all the questions** that you will encounter in the exam. The heading 'Commentary' applies to the specific AO2 requirement of the question (e.g. 'Evaluate' or 'To what extent?').

Marks	Commentary	Analysis	Use of material
12-11	Informed	Thorough	Effective
10-9	Reasonable	Slightly limited	Effective
8-7	Reasonable	Limited	Reasonably effective
6-5	Basic	Limited	Reasonably effective
4-3	Superficial	Rudimentary	Minimal interpretation
2-1	Just discernible	Weak and muddled	Mainly irrelevant
0	Wholly irrelevant	Wholly irrelevant	Wholly irrelevant

Quality of Written Communication (QoWC)

The AQA–A AS Psychology exam also includes **an assessment of your written communication skills**. There are up to two marks awarded in each unit paper. That isn't a great deal, but it helps to know that they are there and how you can make sure you get them! The table below may help you in this:

2 marks	Accurate and clear expression of ideas, a broad range of specialist terms and only minor errors in grammar, punctuation and spelling.
1 mark	Reasonable expression of ideas, a reasonable range of specialist terms and few errors of grammar, punctuation and spelling.
0 marks	Poor expression of ideas, limited use of specialist terms and poor grammar, punctuation and spelling

Exam Tips

■ **Read the questions carefully**, as marks are only available for the specific requirements of the question set. Miss those out and you lose marks; include something irrelevant and you've wasted valuable time.

■ **Make a brief plan** before answering the question. This may be in your head or it may be on paper, but you must know where you are going and how long it will take you to get there. **Time management is absolutely vital**.

■ Sometimes questions ask you to **outline** something. You need to practise doing this as the skill of précis is not as easy as it looks.

■ **Be aware of the difference between AO1 and AO2 skills in questions**. The AO2 component of a question is not just an opportunity for more descriptive content. You must **engage with the question topic** in the required way.

■ **Mind your language**. All exams now carry additional marks for **Quality of Written Communication** (QoWC). This is an assessment of your expression of ideas, use of specialist terms and your grammar, punctuation and spelling.

■ **Use this book as it is intended**. The aim of this book is not to provide you with a set of 'model answers' but to give you skills and insights so you can use your own knowledge and critical skills more effectively in your exam.

Exam Questions

Time allowed: 30 minutes

Answer **one** question. You should attempt all parts of the question you choose.

Question 1

(a) Explain what is meant by the terms 'flashbulb memory', 'repression' and 'reconstructive memory'. [2 marks + 2 marks + 2 marks]

(b) Outline **two** explanations of forgetting in short-term memory. [3 marks + 3 marks]

(c) 'The multi-store model proposed by Atkinson and Shiffrin has been very influential, but it has been criticized for its oversimplification and lack of flexibility.'

To what extent does psychological research support the multi-store model as an adequate explanation of human memory? [18 marks]

Question 2

(a) Describe the main features of an alternative model to the multi-store model. [6 marks]

(b) Describe the procedures *and* findings from **one** study that has investigated the nature of short-term memory. [6 marks]

(c) To what extent does psychological research support the idea that eyewitness testimony is unreliable? [18 marks]

CHOOSING THE BEST QUESTION

Although you only have 30 minutes to answer the question, it is **really important that you take some time to read both questions before you begin to write anything**. You may have been praying for the topic of 'flashbulb memory' to come up in the exam, but don't be tempted to launch into Question 1 simply because you see the magic words in the first line. Your knowledge about flashbulb memory will only gain you a maximum of 2 marks, and there is no further reference to it in the rest of Question 1. **You need to check what is in all parts of both questions before you decide which question provides you with the best opportunity for showing what you know.**

All the topic areas in the 'Cognitive' section will be sampled across the two questions, but this will not necessarily be the case within one question. For example, Question 2 does not include a question based on the subsection of forgetting. This could be an important factor in determining your choice.

The number of marks available for each part of the question is shown in brackets. Although the total number of marks for each question will always add up to 30 and the marks for the last question will always be 18, the way in which they are distributed for parts (a) and (b) differ within questions. You may, for example, prefer to answer Question 1 where the marks are broken down into smaller units (e.g. 2 + 2 + 2 for part (a) and 3 + 3 for part (b)). Alternatively, you may feel that you prefer writing bigger 'chunks' and would rather go for the 6-mark parts in Question 2,

As you read through, be sure to **note the specific requirements of each question**. For example, Question 1 part (b) requires **two explanations** of forgetting in **short-term memory.** You will get no marks here for explanations of forgetting in **long-term memory** or for describing **studies** rather than explanations of forgetting. In Question 2 part (b), you are asked to describe the procedures and findings of a study of the nature of short-term memory, so you would be wasting your time outlining the aims and /or the conclusions as well.

It is very important to read the last part (i.e. part (c)) of each question carefully. Part (c) is worth 18 marks and so you need to look at this carefully before you decide whether to answer Question 1 or 2. This final part of the question requires you to **use AO2 skills as well as AO1**, and so you are being asked to do **rather more than simply describe** material. There are **6** marks available here for AO1, i.e. the ability to demonstrate knowledge and understanding, but **12** marks for AO2. AO2 is a rather different kind of skill, where you are required to show an ability to analyse and evaluate the material. You will need to think carefully about which question will allow you to demonstrate this skill to your best advantage. In this case, the two last questions are very different. **Question 1 requires you to evaluate a specific model** of memory and you will need to have detailed understanding of that particular model and its strengths and weaknesses. You will gain up to 6 marks for the AO1 content (e.g. a brief description of the model and its assumptions), but, to gain the 12 AO2 marks, you are expected to engage with the material in a particular way. In this question, you will need to assess the research which supports the model and to contrast this with research which shows the model to be inadequate. **Question 2 calls for evaluation of the reliability of eyewitness testimony** and perhaps allows you a little more flexibility in the research you choose to discuss because it is not tied into one specific study. You are, however, still required to show AO1 skills for 6 marks (e.g. description of research) and AO2 skills for 12 marks (e.g. assessment of the research in terms of how adequately it sheds light on the reliability of eyewitness testimony).

Tom and Tracey decide to answer Question 1. Their answers are shown next.

Students' answers to Question 1, parts (a) and (b)

(a) Explain what is meant by the terms 'flashbulb memory', 'repression' and 'reconstructive memory'. [2 marks + 2 marks + 2 marks]

TOM'S ANSWER

Vivid memory for an event like Princess Diana dying — something sticks in your mind because it is important. Not remembering something because it is too horrible. Forgetting something.

2/2
1/2
0/2

TRACEY'S ANSWER

Flashbulb memory is when you remember something that is particularly important or unusual. It can be something that is in the newspapers like the death of Princess Diana or it can be something personal to you like your wedding day. You usually remember the details like where you were and who was with you and what the weather was like even after a long time. Repression is to do with Freud. It means pushing something away in your mind. Reconstructive memory means that you have something in your memory but it's not quite accurate – it's changed.

2/2
1/2
1/2

(b) Outline **two** explanations of forgetting in short-term memory.

[3 marks + 3 marks]

TOM'S ANSWER

One explanation of forgetting in STM is displacement. This is where items are pushed out of STM because the capacity is full. STM can only hold a limited number of items at any one time. New items can only enter STM if existing items are displaced. Decay is another explanation. This is where memories simply fade away.

3/3
2/3

TRACEY'S ANSWER

Displacement is a way of forgetting in STM. This means that things already in STM are pushed out to make way for new things.

Decay can also happen which was shown by Peterson and Peterson.

2/3
1/3

How to score full marks

Part (a)

TOM'S ANSWER

Although Tom has given the explanations for the terms in the order they were set out in the question, **he does not make it explicitly clear which term is being explained. It would be better to state the term at the beginning of each explanation so that the examiner is left in no doubt.** You will notice that Tom has not written in proper sentences. As long as the sense is clear, this should not affect his marks for the question. However, **you need to remember that there are marks on each paper for quality of written communication (QoWC), and Tom could be penalized here if he does not write clearly and accurately.** Tom has conveyed an accurate and reasonably detailed explanation of 'flashbulb memory'. It has helped that he has provided a good example, e.g. the death of Princess Diana. **Appropriate examples can often be a useful way of clarifying your explanation.** His explanation of 'repression' is **limited and lacks detail**, but conveys the essence of what is meant by the term and so he gains 1 mark for this. To gain full marks, it would be useful to refer to the unconscious nature of repressed memories or, perhaps, to give an example of the kind of memory that might be repressed. **The last explanation, however, is far too vague** and tells us nothing about the specific nature of 'reconstructive memory', so Tom earns no marks for this.

TRACEY'S ANSWER

Tracey has been a bit more successful on this question. **She has given a detailed and accurate explanation of 'flashbulb memory'.** She, too, has provided good **examples**, and she has conveyed the important information that such memories are vivid, accurate and long-lasting, so earns 2/2. **She has been less clear in her explanation of 'repression', and this is why she has scored only 1 mark.** The term is certainly associated with Freud and involves suppressing information, but she has not explained why such memories are 'pushed away' (i.e., because they provoke anxiety). **Her third explanation shows some understanding of the term 'reconstructive memory', but it also lacks detail and scores only 1 mark. For full marks, she needs to explain that we do not store information passively, but, instead, weave it into our existing stores of knowledge and past experience (schemas).** When we later come to recall this information, it is often distorted.

Part (b)

TOM'S ANSWER

The first explanation given by Tom is **accurate and detailed**. He has clearly identified a method of forgetting – displacement – and given a **full explanation** of why this occurs and so he gains 3/3. He has also identified a second method of forgetting in STM and explained that this means that memories fade away. However, this is rather limited and he would have scored full marks if he had explained about the **important role of rehearsal in the prevention of decay**. As it is, he can only earn 2/3.

TRACEY'S ANSWER

Tracey has also correctly identified two methods of forgetting in STM. However, she has not given the same amount of detail as Tom. She has not, for example, explained that **displacement is a direct result of the limited capacity of STM** and so only earns 2/3 for this explanation. Her second explanation is little more than an identification of a method. The reference to Peterson and Peterson is pretty meaningless on its own without any **explanation of what they showed** in their experiment. As it stands, this answer can only gain 1/3.

Don't forget ...

- If asked to explain three **different** terms, make sure that you set your answer out **clearly** so that the examiner knows which term is being explained.

- Explanations of terms **require some degree of detail**. You will not get marks for vague answers.

- **Make sure that you understand** what is meant by terms such as '**study**'. If you are asked to describe a study, you will gain no marks for describing a theory or an anecdote.

- **Use examples**. They can sometimes help to clarify your explanation of a particular term.

- **Read the questions carefully**. If you are asked to provide an outline of **factors**, you will gain **no credit for descriptions of studies**.

- If you are asked to **outline** two factors that might influence, for example, eyewitness testimony, you must make sure that you demonstrate **how** the factors exert their influence. It is not enough simply to identify an appropriate factor.

Tom's answer to Question 1, part (c)

(c) 'The multi-store model proposed by Atkinson and Shiffrin has been very influential, but it has been criticized for its oversimplification and lack of flexibility.'

To what extent does psychological research support the multi-store model as an adequate explanation of human memory? [18 marks]

> **Tom is wasting time here – there is no time to write a broad introduction to the topic of memory. The last sentence would earn AO1 marks.**

Memory is very important to humans. Without it, they would not be able to remember anything about themselves or how to do anything. A man called Clive Wearing lost his memory after an illness and it was like being in a living hell. Lots of psychologists have studied memory. The first people to come up with a theory were Atkinson and Shiffrin. They called it the multi-store model but it is also called the modal model. It has three parts which are sensory memory, short-term memory and long-term memory.

> **This could be a good AO2 point supporting the Atkinson and Shiffrin (A & S) idea that there is a different store for each sensory modality. Unfortunately, Tom does not make this point *explicit*.**

Sensory memory can only hold things for a very brief time. Sperling showed that it lasts for about 1/2 a second if you look at letters, but someone else found that it lasts for 2 seconds if you hear sounds.

> **This is simply a description of Miller's findings. How does this relate to the A & S model?**

Short-term memory holds about 7 items. This was found out by Miller, but he said that we could hold more if we put them in chunks.

> **At last! Tom is beginning to introduce material to *support* the multi-store theory.**
> **Another evaluative point. Tom has introduced a different theory (levels of processing) to *criticize* the multi-store model.**

Atkinson and Shiffrin say that we have to repeat things over and over if we want to keep them in short-term memory. If we repeat them enough, they will go into long-term memory but if we cannot repeat them, they are lost. Brown and Peterson gave people nonsense words to remember but did not let them repeat them. They forgot them very quickly which shows that repeating is important. Craik and Lockhart criticized this. They said that repeating on its own is not enough – you need to process the words and the deeper you process them, the more likely you are to remember them.

> **Amnesia studies can be useful to evaluate the A & S model, but Tom does not explain *how* and he does not demonstrate a good understanding of the amnesia research.**

People with amnesia support the multi-store model. Clive Wearing can remember things at this moment (short-term memory) but he can't remember the past (long-term memory). HM who had an operation for epilepsy was the same. KF who had a motorbike accident was different, though. He had a bad short-term memory but his long-term memory seemed all right. This is difficult for Atkinson and Shiffrin to explain.

AO1 = 4/6   AO2 = 5/12   Total = 9/18

Tracey's answer to Question 1, part (c)

(c) 'The multi-store model proposed by Atkinson and Shiffrin has been very influential, but it has been criticized for its oversimplification and lack of flexibility.'

To what extent does psychological research support the multi-store model as an adequate explanation of human memory? [18 marks]

> **This is a good start. Tracey is setting out the basic assumptions of the multi-store model and will earn AO1 marks for this.**

Atkinson and Shiffrin put forward the multi-store model which is a structural model of memory. They thought that memory was divided up into 3 separate stores called sensory, short-term and long-term memory. There is a lot of support for this idea.

> **Tracey is describing Sperling's and Treisman's findings (AO1) but using the material *effectively* to support the model (AO2).**

Sperling investigated sensory memory and found that it held visual information for only about 50 milliseconds. If it is not passed on to STM in that time, it will be lost. Treisman, while researching attention, found that sensory memory for auditory information lasts a bit longer – approx. 2 seconds. This fits the multi-store model in which sensory memory is thought to consist of different stores for different senses.

> **This is a good point – it shows how the evidence that is cited is *relevant* i.e. there is empirical support for the idea of different structures within memory. There is relevant AO1 and AO2 material here.**

STM and LTM seem to work differently in several ways. For example, Miller showed that STM can only hold 7 + or −2 items, but it seems that LTM can hold as much as you want. The two stores also use different coding methods according to Baddeley. STM prefers acoustic coding and LTM prefers semantic coding. Finally, STM only lasts for a few seconds and LTM lasts for ever. These differences show that the two stores must be separate.

> **Another good point. Tracey contrasts the unitary store in the A & S model with the more complex nature of the working memory model.**

Not everyone agrees with this. Baddeley thinks the model is too simple. He put forward the idea of working memory which allows STM to do different tasks. Atkinson and Shiffrin said STM was just a storehouse.

> **Now she contrasts the multi-store model with the levels of processing model, although this point is not well developed.**

Atkinson and Shiffrin thought that we transfer information into LTM by rehearsing it. Other psychologists think that deep processing is necessary to transfer information.

> **Is Tracey running out of time? She should not start asking questions. She is hinting at an important point here, but she does not *develop* it. The appraisal of the model as 'good' and 'fair' is a bit vague and not supported by evidence. The reference to the amnesia research is relevant, but poorly explained.**

Why is it that we remember some things better than others? The multi-store model does not explain this. I think it has been a very good model and it is very fair but there is a lot it does not explain like some patients with amnesia who are able to use LTM without going through STM.

AO1 = 6/6   AO2 = 8/12   Total = 14/18

How to score full marks for part (c)

🎯 Avoid irrelevant material

You will have approximately 18 minutes to write this part of the answer, so you do not have time to waste. It is important to engage with the question from the beginning. Do not waste time with a lengthy introductory paragraph that does little to address the question (as Tom did). In this example, it is not necessary to explain what is meant by memory, nor to give a history of research. **You need to engage from the outset with the adequacy of the multi-store model.**

🎯 Use specialist vocabulary

You need to write grammatically and in complete sentences, but Tom has wasted time in writing out the terms 'short-term memory' and 'long-term memory' several times. **It is perfectly acceptable to use the abbreviations STM and LTM.** It is important in this type of question to be able to **express ideas succinctly**. It often helps if you are able to use **specialist terms** and can remember the names of **key researchers**, as this can condense the number of words required. For example, **Tom could have dealt with sensory memory more economically and made an evaluative point at the same time** by saying: 'According to Atkinson and Shiffrin, there is a store for each of the *sensory modalities*. This was confirmed by *Sperling*, who investigated the *iconic store*, and *Treisman*, who found evidence for an *echoic store*. One way that shows that they operate independently is that they have different *durations*.' (Specialist terms and names shown in italics.)

🎯 Make your evaluative points clear

Tom has also made the mistake of **describing facts without making them specifically relevant** to the multi-store model and **without drawing appropriate conclusions**. Although 6 marks are available for descriptive material, it must be clearly relevant to the question. For example, his short paragraph about the capacity of STM is not really linked to the multi-store model and provides neither support nor criticism, so can gain little credit. Tom should have made it clear that it is an assumption of the multi-store model that STM is limited in capacity and that this has been supported by Miller's research into the serial digit span. Tracey deals with this better by introducing her paragraph with the sentence: 'STM and LTM seem to work differently in several ways.' In this way, she signals that she is **evaluating** a key concept in the multi-store model i.e. that STM and LTM are separate and operate differently.

🎯 Consider strengths and weaknesses: strengths

In this type of question, you need to think about the strengths and weaknesses of the model in order to demonstrate its adequacy as an explanation. One positive aspect is that it was one of the first testable models of memory and it provided a basic framework that could be expanded by later researchers – for example, the working memory model as an extension of the concept of STM (**Baddeley and Hitch**) and the idea of semantic/episodic/procedural memory (**Tulving**) as a way of understanding LTM. There is support for the model in terms of its fundamental distinction between STM and LTM. Evidence that could be cited here is **Murdock's** free recall studies, and also any studies that show a distinction between the methods of operation of STM and LTM, e.g. **Miller's** research into the capacity of STM, or **Baddeley's** studies into the relative encoding strategies of the two stores. **Case studies of people with amnesia induced by brain damage could be used effectively to support the distinction between STM and LTM.** The role of rehearsal, which is central to the **Atkinson and Shiffrin** model, could be supported by research based on the **Brown–Peterson** technique and could be contrasted with the levels of processing approach, which stressed the nature rather than the amount of rehearsal.

Consider strengths and weaknesses: weaknesses

You have been asked in this question to assess the **extent** to which psychological research supports the multi-store model, but **this does not mean that you must only focus on evidence that is in favour of the model. By assessing the extent, you also need to consider the counter-evidence.** Weaknesses of the model include the fact that it is **too simple** – Atkinson and Shiffrin seem to make the assumption that all material is remembered in the same way and **they do not take into account the fact that certain things are easier to recall** (e.g. film stars' names rather than psychology researchers' names!). **Other theories, such as levels of processing, can explain this better.** There is also **evidence** to suggest that the **flow of information through the system is not always one way**, as Atkinson and Shiffrin suggested. For example, visually presented letters registering on sensory memory are translated into an acoustic code for access to STM – this can only happen if the individual is first able to obtain information about letter shapes and sounds from LTM. **The idea that LTM can only be accessed through STM has also been undermined by the case study of KF**, whose STM capacity was grossly impaired but who seemed able to transfer new items into LTM. **The role of the STM as a simple, unitary storage unit has been questioned by Baddeley and Hitch,** who have produced evidence to support the idea of a multi-component STM. The emphasis on structural components in the multi-store model has been criticized by **Craik and Lockhart,** who have shown that **processes might be more important than structures**.

Don't forget ...

- The last part of each question is **worth 18 marks**. Allow yourself **enough time** (approximately 18 minutes) to answer this in sufficient depth.

- The last part of the question will be assessing your ability to show **knowledge and understanding** (AO1 or Assessment Objective 1) **and** your ability to **analyse and evaluate** theories, concepts, studies and methods (AO2 or Assessment Objective 2). You will not gain many marks here by simply describing theories or research. You need to make sure that all your material, whether descriptive or evaluative, is made **clearly relevant to the question**.

- Remember that you need to **consider both sides of the argument** when you are asked to assess the extent to which a theory/model is supported.

- **Two marks are allocated for the quality of written communication** across the whole paper. It is worthwhile trying to write clearly and accurately, using specialist terms correctly.

Human memory

Human memory refers to the **mental processes** we use in order to acquire, store, retrieve and use our knowledge about the world.

Short-term memory and long-term memory

Short-term memory (STM) is a system for storing information for brief periods of time. For some researchers (e.g. **Atkinson and Shiffrin**), it is seen as a temporary storage box for information. For others (e.g. **Baddeley and Hitch**), it is seen as a more complex system consisting of different working components. It is generally accepted that the capacity of STM is limited, although whether it is limited by the number of items it can hold (e.g. **Miller**) or by time restraints (e.g. Baddeley and Hitch) is a matter for discussion. **Long-term memory (LTM)**, in contrast, is thought to have an infinite capacity and is able to store a huge range of information over long periods of time. There are several theories that have been proposed which attempt to explain human memory processes. The **multi-store model** mainly associated with Atkinson and Shiffrin focuses on the **structural aspects of memory** and distinguishes between sensory, short-term and long-term memory. These structures are thought to differ from one another in terms of capacity, duration and encoding. Baddeley and Hitch focused on the STM, but thought that it was a much more complex system than Atkinson and Shiffrin. Their **working memory model** comprises a set of slave-systems under the control of a central executive. A rather different model was proposed by **Craik and Lockhart**, who believed that the crucial factor in laying down new memories is the amount and depth of processing they receive. For this reason, their model is called the **levels of processing theory**.

Forgetting

We cannot remember everything that enters the memory system and psychologists have been interested in investigating some of the reasons why we forget. Forgetting seems to occur rather differently in the two main stores. In **STM**, the main mechanisms for forgetting are **decay** and **displacement**, whereas in **LTM**, it seems that **retrieval failure** and **interference** are the most likely reasons why we forget. Sometimes our ability to remember can be influenced by our emotional state. **Flashbulb memories** are vivid, accurate and long-lasting memories for events which have particular significance for us. In this case, **emotional involvement** appears to improve our recall. **Freud**, however, believed that **strong emotions could sometimes interfere with accurate recall**. He described **repression** as an unconscious process whereby a distressing memory or impulse is excluded from conscious awareness.

Critical issue: Eyewitness testimony

One particular area of interest for memory researchers is the field of eyewitness testimony. Although people are sometimes able to recall events with high degrees of accuracy, **eyewitness testimony can be unreliable**. One possible reason is that memories are **distorted or reconstructed**. **Bartlett** first introduced the idea of **reconstructive memory**, whereby we store memories in terms of our past knowledge and experience (schemas). A more recent researcher in this field is **Elizabeth Loftus**, who has been particularly concerned with the effects of **misleading information** provided after the event.

Harrow College
Harrow Weald, Learning Centre
Brookshill, Harrow Weald
HA3 6RR
020 8909 6248

21

Question for you to try

Examiner's hints

- In part (a), you are **only** required to write about one alternative to the multi-store model. Do not waste time by writing a general introduction about other models of memory. You can choose any alternative, but it is likely that you will have studied either the Working Memory model of Baddeley and Hitch, or the Levels of Processing Model of Craik and Lockhart.
- Part (a) only assesses AO1 skills – you will be **wasting time** if you include an evaluation of the model in your answer.
- Take care that you choose a study in part (b) where you are able to describe **both** the procedures **and** the findings. You can choose **any** study related to STM, for example on capacity, duration or encoding.
- **Make sure** that you choose a study for part (b) that is concerned with STM – you will gain no marks for a study on LTM.
- In part (c), you are required to demonstrate **both AO1 and AO2** skills. However, bear in mind the **6/12 mark** split between AO1 and AO2 – you will not gain many marks simply by describing research studies. **You must engage with the material and use the examples of research effectively to consider the reliability of eyewitness testimony**.

(a) Describe the main features of an alternative model to the multi-store model.

[6 marks]

(b) Describe the procedures *and* findings from **one** study that has investigated the nature of short-term memory.   [6 marks]

(c) To what extent does psychological research support the idea that eyewitness testimony is unreliable?   [18 marks]

Answers are given on pp. 80–81.

2 Attachments in Development

Exam Questions

Time allowed: 30 minutes

Answer **one** question. You should attempt all parts of the question you choose.

Question 1

(a) Outline the findings of **one** study of cross-cultural variations in attachments and give **one** evaluation of this study. [3 marks + 3 marks]

(b) Describe **one** explanation of attachment. [6 marks]

(c) Outline and evaluate research (theories **and/or** studies) into privation. [18 marks]

Question 2

(a) Explain what is meant by the following terms: 'maternal deprivation'; 'privation'; 'secure attachment'. [2 marks + 2 marks + 2 marks]

(b) Outline the development of attachments. [6 marks]

(c) Consider the possible benefits and/or disadvantages of day care for children's social and/or cognitive development. [18 marks]

CHOOSING THE BEST QUESTION

Be sure to read both questions carefully before you start writing. In this way you will select the question that will enable you to score the highest marks. **Do a rough calculation to work out how many marks in each question you think you can achieve**. Don't just make up your mind on the basis of the first couple of parts in each question. Which of the questions above would you choose?

Although all topic areas in 'Attachments in Development' will be sampled over the two questions, this will not necessarily occur within any one question. **Take care not to** rush into answering because the first couple of parts are about an area you particularly enjoyed. Later parts may ask you about another area altogether. Of course, sometimes a question will deal with only one or two topics.

Whether or not you have preferences for individual topics, you will still need to **read each part of the two questions carefully and note their specific requirements**. If you prefer to give fairly short answers, then Question 2 may be more attractive to you since part (a) is divided into three sections rather than two, as in Question 1, part (a). However, if you are more confident about describing an **explanation** of attachment than outlining its development, Question 1 may be a better option since 6 marks are allocated to this in part (b).

 It is **important to look at part (c)** of each question before choosing which to answer because this part of the question is worth more marks than the other two parts combined. Remember that **part (c) of the question (worth 18 marks) requires both AO1 and AO2 skills**. That is, you are asked to do more than just describe material relevant to the area. You are also asked to **engage** with the material in a specific way. In Question 1 you are asked to 'outline and evaluate' research into privation. Remember that 6 marks are available for AO1 content (that is, outlining – briefly describing – the research) and 12 marks for AO2 content (that is, evaluating the research outlined. This

means providing an informed commentary on research into privation). Therefore, although some AO1 content is required it is **how you engage with it** that will determine how many AO2 marks you receive. Question 2, part (c) asks you to 'consider…' the possible benefits and/or disadvantages of day care for children's social and/or cognitive development. Again, there are 6 marks available for AO1 content (e.g. what are the possible benefits or disadvantages of day care for development) and 12 marks for AO2 content. One way of 'considering' material in an AO2 manner is to examine the degree to which research findings support or challenge an assertion. **Choose the question that gives you the chance to score the highest mark overall** and remember that **really high marks are awarded when material is used effectively**.

Martin and Mary decide to answer Question 1. Their answers are shown next.

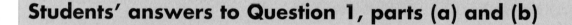

Students' answers to Question 1, parts (a) and (b)

(a) Outline the findings of **one** study of cross-cultural variations in attachments and give **one** evaluation of this study. [3 marks + 3 marks]

MARTIN'S ANSWER

A big study that compared lots of small studies found that in most countries, most babies are securely attached and so there is not much variation.

(1/3)

Some psychologists have criticised using the strange situation in these studies because children in some countries became very upset and so it was unethical to use the strange situation.

(2/3)

MARY'S ANSWER

Mary Ainsworth developed the Strange Situation where a child is left on their own in a strange room. Then a stranger comes in and tries to be friendly to the child who is crying because the mother has left. In one study in Japan, most babies were securely attached, the same as in America but no babies were avoidant-insecure, unlike in America where 21% were in this category.

(2/3)

It is difficult to understand other cultures and so findings from cross-cultural research are confusing.

(1/3)

(b) Describe **one** explanation of attachment.   [6 marks]

MARTIN'S ANSWER

Bowlby's theory of attachment is based on the theory of evolution. Babies become attached to their mother by instinct because this keeps them safe from danger and teaches them how to make relationships later in life. If an infant does not form an attachment they may have trouble with relationships later on. He said that babies become attached to only one person. Other people have criticized Bowlby's explanation. They say that babies can be attached to lots of people and that parents teach their children to love them.

$\frac{3}{6}$

MARY'S ANSWER

Behaviourists claim that conditioning causes attachment. If you are rewarded for doing something you are more likely to do it again. Babies like the mother best because she provides food.

$\frac{2}{6}$

How to score full marks

Part (a)

🎯 MARTIN'S ANSWER

Martin's answer refers to Van Ijendoorn and Kroonenberg meta-analyses of 32 studies carried out in different countries using the Strange Situation. This is OK as it counts as 'one' study for this question. However, Martin's answer is **basic** and **flawed**. Most babies were indeed found to be securely attached (and for this point Martin earns 1 mark) but the meta-analyses revealed interesting variations in insecure attachments between cultures. Martin provides a **generally accurate** evaluation but it **lacks detail**. To gain full marks, you could explain, for example, what it was about the Strange Situation procedure that caused Japanese infants to become very distressed.

🎯 MARY'S ANSWER

Mary's answer earns 2 marks because it provides **generally accurate** findings from a well-known Japanese study (Takahashi 1990). **For full marks, you would need to give accurate and detailed findings** (e.g. 68% of Japanese and 65% of American infants were securely attached) and give the percentage for resistant-insecure as well as avoidant-insecure infants). The details about the procedure used in the Strange Situation are not asked for in the question and so attract no marks. Mary's evaluation of the study is **too basic** to attract more than 1 mark. She makes a general evaluative point about cross-cultural research but does not relate it to attachments. For full marks you could explain why 'avoidant behaviour', as classified in the Strange Situation, might mean different things in different cultures.

Part (b)

There are several explanations for attachment that you could use (e.g. learning theory, social learning theory, psychodynamic theory, Bowlby's theory) to answer the question.

MARTIN'S ANSWER

Martin chooses Bowlby's theory but his answer lacks detail, although it is generally accurate. Therefore he gains only 3/6. Note, however, that Bowlby did not claim that infants become attached to only one person, but rather that they have an innate tendency to form a strong, qualitatively different bond (attachment) with one individual, usually the mother. This is called his monotropy hypothesis. **For full marks you should describe the main features of Bowlby's explanation**: attachment as adaptive (i.e., it increases the infant's chances of survival and reproduction); the role of social releasers (such as crying) that produce a care-giving reaction from another person; the sensitive period for its development; proximity seeking by child; use of parent as safe base for exploration; and how the first attachment provides a template for future relationships. **Note that Martin gains no marks for giving criticisms of Bowlby's theory**, because the question asks for a **description** of one explanation, **not** for an evaluation.

MARY'S ANSWER

Mary's description of conditioning as an explanation of attachment is **basic and lacks detail**. Therefore, the answer earns only 2/6. **Ensure that you have a good grasp of the explanation you choose. For full marks you need to show clearly how behaviourists have explained attachment in terms of classical and operant conditioning**. For instance, the way a mother becomes associated with the pleasure an infant feels when it is fed is an example of classical conditioning. According to operant conditioning principles, rewarded behaviours are repeated. Instinctively, a baby is 'driven' to seek food when hungry. After feeding, the hunger 'drive' is reduced and this is rewarding. Therefore, when the baby is hungry again it repeats the behaviour (e.g. crying) that leads to the drive reduction. Since the mother provides the food (a primary reinforcer) to reduce the hunger drive, she becomes a secondary reinforcer (by the process of classical conditioning) and the infant strives to stay close to her. Thereby, the infant becomes attached.

Don't forget ...

- If you are asked to outline or describe **more than one** feature or explanation, be sure to do so. Try to do each in appropriate detail, as each will be marked independently.

- If asked to describe **one** explanation, write about only one!

- Do not spend time giving **evaluations** if you are asked only to **describe**.

- **When asked for a description, provide some detail**. A definition or short sentence is not enough. However, remember that you have only got three minutes approximately for a 3-mark answer, and six minutes for a 6-mark answer.

Martin's answer to Question 1, part (c)

(c) Outline and evaluate research (theories **and/or** studies) into privation.   [18 marks]

> **This is a good opening paragraph, showing that Martin understands the precise meaning of the term 'privation'. It sets the scene to describe research on the effects of institutional care.**

Privation refers to what happens when a child never has the opportunity to form an attachment. This might happen when a child is orphaned or unwanted and placed in an institution.

> **This is quite a good, though not very detailed, account of Hodges and Tizard's study and so gains some AO1 credit. Martin gains AO2 credit by interpreting the success of the adopted children in terms of privation effects being 'reversible'. However, he fails to point out that while adopted children attached closely to their adoptive parents they still had problems with social relationships outside their immediate families and so their early privations might have had some lasting effects. This type of commentary would have earned more AO2 marks.**

Hodges and Tizard conducted a longitudinal study on children who were put in care before they were 4 months old. They measured how well the children were doing when they were 4, 8 and 16 years old. Some children had been adopted, some returned to their real families and others stayed in the institution. Adopted children did best, showing that early privation need not have lasting effects.

> **Some good AO1 and AO2 content here. Martin also could have mentioned the problems that arise in interpreting case studies (e.g. difficulties with generalising from them) and so have gained more AO2 marks**

The case of the Czech twin boys shows that privation effects can be overcome as long as the privated children have good care later on. Koluchova reported on twin boys who were abused by their cruel stepmother and unintelligent father. They were kept in a cellar until they were found at age 7. They were in bad physical shape and had poor speech but they had had each other and maybe that helped them recover when they were looked after later in a caring foster home.

> **More relevant and accurate AO1 content but again Martin misses the opportunity to evaluate the case study method.**

Unfortunately Genie, who was also neglected and abused, was kept alone until she was found at 13 years old. She had been tied to a potty and so could not walk properly and did not speak. Although she received lots of therapy and was fostered, she never recovered from her early privations and did not develop proper speech.

> **Good conclusion, expanding on the earlier evaluative point about the possibility of reversing the bad effects of privation.**

In conclusion, some research into privation suggests that children who have experienced privation early in life can recover well if they are well looked after later on. But children like Genie, who are privated for a long time, may never recover, especially if they do not get sympathetic care.

AO1 = 4/6   AO2 = 7/12   Total = 11/18

> **Overall, there is a disproportionate amount of AO1 compared to AO2 in Martin's answer. Remember that twice as many marks are available for AO2 as for AO1 points.**

Mary's answer to Question 1, part (c)

(c) Outline and evaluate research (theories **and/or** studies) into privation. [18 marks]

> **Excellent opener, explaining what she understands by the term 'privation' and setting out the structure for the answer to follow. Remember that 'research' refers to both theory as well as studies.**

> **Mary provides accurate AO1 content about this well-known study of privation.**

> **Some relevant AO2 commentary here but Mary should relate it more explicitly to the question set. It is a pity that Mary does not evaluate the research method used in this study (e.g. the problem of attrition in longitudinal studies, the inevitable lack of random allocation of children to the different treatment groups). (See p.29)**

> **A concise AO2 point about limitations of case studies introduced here.**

> **A good balance of AO1 and AO2 content. Mary is running out of time and sensibly cuts short the AO1 detail to allow time for informed AO2 commentary.**

Some psychologists believe that privated children (those who never get the chance to form a primary attachment) will suffer long-term, irreversible effects. Other psychologists think that the negative effects of privation can sometimes be overcome.

Research carried out into the effects of institutionalisation provides evidence for both points of view. Hodges and Tizard's longitudinal study looked at children who, since infancy, had been in an institution where they had no chance to become attached to an adult. They then compared the children who were adopted with those who were restored to their own family. They found that the adopted children formed closer relationships with their parents. Both adopted and restored children had difficulty forming relationships at school.

According to Hodges and Tizard, adopted children were loved and wanted by their families, who made special efforts to help them overcome their problems, and that is why the children formed close attachments to them. Restored children received less favourable treatment. Both sets of children, however, found it difficult to cope socially when other people were not making allowances for them and therefore they had problems.

Case studies have also been used to research the effects of early privation but case studies have their own problems as information is gathered in retrospect and there may be memory distortions that make the findings unreliable.

Two case studies (one about Czech twin boys and another about six war orphans) found that children could recover from severe privations early in life if they were given excellent care and therapy later on. However, in both these studies, the children were not completely isolated during their time of privation and may have developed attachments to each other even if they did not become attached to an adult. Therefore, we could say that they are not true studies of privation. Genie, on the other hand, who was kept in near solitude until she was 13, failed to develop normally after she was found. This suggests that being unable to form any attachments in early life may have lasting, irreversible, negative effects. Genie, of course, suffered multiple privations not just the lack of an attachment.

AO1 = 5/6   AO2 = 10/12   Total = 15/18

How to score full marks for part (c)

🎯 Answer the question set

With 18 marks to earn in a short period, it is important not to waste time. **Give only the information that is asked for**. Remember to **link all your points clearly to the question**. Always bear in mind that both **AO1 and AO2 skills** are required in this part of the question (see pages 8–11).

🎯 Structuring your answer

Your task is to **outline and then evaluate** research into privation. Make sure that you structure your answer so that it reflects the 6/12 split between AO1 and AO2 marks for this part of the question.

➤ AO1 content

An outline of some of the following studies of privation would provide suitable AO1 content: Hodges and Tizard's (1989) study of ex-institutional children; Rutter's (1998) study of Romanian orphans; Harlow and Harlow's (1962) maternal deprivation studies using monkeys (note that the question does not require you to use only human research); case studies of severe privation, e.g. those by Koluchova (1976), Curtis (1989), and Freud and Dann (1951). Remember that an outline of a study should include the **main findings**. Avoid describing procedures at length.

➤ AO2 content: evaluate the research by analysing findings

You can use a number of different ways to evaluate research. For example, you may analyse and comment on the findings of the research described for AO1. You might point out that some research suggests that the negative effects of early privation are irreversible no matter how much remedial help is provided. On the other hand, other research findings indicate that, with appropriate help, children can make a good recovery, despite having suffered extreme privation. It is OK to **consider cognitive as well as social development** when answering this question and worth pointing out that **some findings are not clear cut**. While the adopted ex-institutional children in Hodges and Tizard's study had close relationships with parents and did quite well academically, they found it difficult to sustain friendships. **By analysing the reasons for this you would gain AO2 marks.**

➤ AO2 content: evaluate the methods used to carry out the research

You could do this by pointing out that **longitudinal studies** run into problems when some of the original participants are no longer available (called **attrition**) so that the final sample may be biased. Hodges and Tizard's study also encountered another problem. Obviously the researchers were not the ones to decide which children would be adopted and which restored to their natural families. This raises the question as to whether children who were already more socially orientated (e.g. had a tendency to smile more) would be more likely to be adopted. If this was a factor then the allocation to conditions would have been biased and might have affected the findings.

You could use any of the following points to **evaluate case studies** of children who have experienced extreme privation:

- Case studies are valuable because they allow us insight into exceptional cases that could not be studied any other way.
- However, the contents are selective, compiled retrospectively and may be difficult to interpret.
- Case studies also often use information from unstructured interviews and these are prone to memory distortions.

Don't forget ...

- The **last part** of all AS questions (except for 'Research Methods') is **worth 18 marks**, so allow yourself adequate time to answer it in sufficient depth.

- This last part of the question will be assessing your **knowledge and understanding** of psychology (AO1 or Assessment Objective 1) and your ability to **analyse and evaluate** this material **in a clear and effective manner** (AO2 or Assessment Objective 2).

- **Two marks are allocated for the quality of written communication** shown in a paper. It is worthwhile trying to write clearly and accurately, using specialist terms correctly.

Key points to remember

Attachments in development
Attachment is a **strong, reciprocal, emotional tie that develops over time between an infant and a primary caregiver**. Its development depends upon the **interaction** of the two people. Infants are probably born with an innate tendency to develop an attachment.

Development and variety of attachments
Schaffer and Emerson proposed four phases in the **development of attachment**: pre-attachment, attachment-in-the-making, clear-cut attachment and multiple attachments. Some researchers have questioned the ages at which these stages occur. One of the most investigated **individual differences** in attachment concerns security/insecurity. **Ainsworth** studied the security of attachments using the **Strange Situation** and found that most infants were securely attached, while about 15 per cent were described as insecure avoidant and another 15 per cent as insecure ambivalent. An infant's **type of attachment** is thought to depend upon the **warmth and responsiveness of the caregiver** and to some extent upon the **innate temperament** of the infant. Attachments vary **across cultures**, although research seems to indicate that secure attachments are important in many cultures. The use of the Strange Situation across cultures and subcultures to assess the security of attachment has been criticized. Different **explanations of attachment** have been proposed. These include learning theory, psychodynamic theory and Bowlby's theory of attachment as an adaptive process.

Critical issue: Day care
Day care is the term used to describe the **care given to pre-school children by people other than a parent**. On the whole, research findings support the claim that day care causes no harm to development, and some children seem to benefit possibly because the day care compensates for the lack of opportunities at home.
Attachments to parents do not seem to be affected by day care. The **quality** of day care is important and can be improved by providing adequate resources, keeping low staff turnover, having low child–staff ratios, and training staff to be responsive to children's needs.

Deprivation and privation
Deprivation is the **loss** of something. In this context, it refers to a situation where a child is deprived of the love of its primary attachment figure. **Privation** is the **lack** of something. In this case, it refers to a situation where no attachment has ever been formed. According to **Bowlby's maternal deprivation hypothesis**, children who are unable to develop a continuous relationship with a mother figure are likely to experience difficulty with later relationships. **Critics of Bowlby** argue that children who are unable to form such an attachment with a mother figure are likely also to suffer other deprivations. **Rutter** also points out that even if there is an association between lack of attachment and later problems with relationships, this does **not** mean there is a cause-and-effect link. Family discord may have led to the maternal deprivation and the subsequent problems. **Longitudinal studies** of ex-institutional children and **individual case studies** of children who have experienced severe privation suggest **that the effects of privation may be reversed when good-quality emotional care is provided at a young enough age**.

Question for you to try

(a) Explain what is meant by the following terms: 'maternal deprivation'; 'privation'; 'secure attachment'.

[2 marks + 2 marks + 2 marks]

(b) Outline the development of attachments.

[6 marks]

(c) Consider the possible benefits and/or disadvantages of day care for children's social and/or cognitive development. [18 marks]

Answers are given on pp. 82–83.

Exam Questions

Time allowed: 30 minutes

Answer **one** question. You should attempt all parts of the question you choose.

Question 1

(a) What is meant by the terms 'stress', 'stressor' and 'stress management'?

[2 marks + 2 marks + 2 marks]

(b) Describe **one** physiological approach to stress management. [6 marks]

(c) To what extent are the effects of stress modified by gender differences?

[18 marks]

Question 2

(a) Outline **two** ways in which the body responds to stress. [3 marks + 3 marks]

(b) Describe the procedures and conclusions of **one** research study that has investigated the role of the workplace as a source of stress. [6 marks]

(c) Outline and evaluate **two or more** psychological approaches to stress management. [18 marks]

CHOOSING THE BEST QUESTION

Be sure to read both questions carefully before you start writing. In this way you will select the question that will enable you to score the highest marks. **Do a rough calculation to work out how many marks in each question you think you can achieve.** Don't just make up your mind on the basis of the first couple of parts in each question. Which of the questions above would you choose?

Although all topic areas in physiological psychology (i.e., 'Stress as a bodily response', 'Sources of stress' and 'Stress management') will be sampled over the two questions, this will not necessarily occur within any one question. **Take care not to rush into answering a question just because you feel you can manage the first part or first couple of parts.** It is easy, in the stress of an examination, to misread or misinterpret the exact requirements of a question. **A couple of quiet minutes reading and thinking about which question you might choose will pay dividends later** (i.e., you won't get halfway into a question and then realize you can't answer the latter parts).

You may have a preference for one topic rather than another (for example, 'Sources of stress' rather than 'Stress as a bodily response'). **This does not mean that the question that contains this topic is overall the most profitable in terms of the total number of marks that you might achieve.** Sometimes you have to forgo a favourite topic because the other parts of the question are not ones that you feel you can answer well. **You will still need to read each part of the two questions carefully and note their specific requirements** in order to make this decision. In Question 2, for example, part (b) asks you to describe the **procedures** and **conclusions** from one study that has investigated the role of the workplace as a source of stress. If you know nothing about the procedures of a study in this area or can't work out the conclusions, then this is clearly not the question for you!

It is very important to look at part (c) of each question before choosing which to answer. The final part of each question requires both AO1 **and** AO2 skills, therefore you are being asked to do **more than simply describe material** that is relevant to the area. You are being asked to **engage** with the material in a specific way. In question 1, you are asked 'to what extent…'

which requires you to weigh up the evidence that the effects of stress really are modified by gender differences. Remember that **6 marks** are available for the AO1 content (e.g. ways in which the effects of stress have been shown to be modified by gender differences) and **12 marks** for the AO2 content. So, although **some** AO1 content is required, it is **what you do with it** that will determine how many of the AO2 marks on offer that you receive. Question 2, on the other hand, offers very clear advice about what is required in your answer. The AO1 content is clearly indicated by the use of 'outline' and the AO2 content by the use of the term 'evaluate'. The only uncertainty arises over the choice of 'two' or 'more than two' psychological approaches to stress management. There is no advantage to covering more than two unless you know very little about each approach, so need to flesh out your answer by covering lots of different approaches. **Beware the superficial response** however, and always include sufficient detail in your chosen approaches. Make sure you are fully aware of what constitutes a psychological approach, and don't mix them up with physiological approaches to stress management.

Matthew and Parveen decide to answer Question 1. Their answers are shown next.

Students' answers to Question 1, parts (a) and (b)

(a) What is meant by the terms 'stress', 'stressor' and 'stress management'?

[2 marks + 2 marks + 2 marks]

MATTHEW'S ANSWER

Stress means when you are stressed.
A stressor is something that causes stress.
Stress management is how you deal with stress. For example, some people deal with stress by going to counselling or taking anti-anxiety drugs.

0/2
1/2
2/2

PARVEEN'S ANSWER

Stress may refer to a lack of fit between the perceived demands of the situation and the person's perceived ability to cope.

2/2

A stressor is something in the environment (such as examinations) that produces a stress response in a person.

2/2

This refers to the different ways in which people attempt to cope with the effects of stress.

2/2

(b) Describe **one** physiological approach to stress management. [6 marks]

MATTHEW'S ANSWER

One way in which people deal with stress is to take drugs such as beta-blockers which work by altering the way that the brain works. These are commonly taken by musicians and snooker players. Other types of drug are librium and valium which alter the brain's chemistry and so lower the levels of stress experienced by the person. Drugs like librium and valium can make people dependent on them if they are taken for a long period of time so should only be used for short periods of time.

3/6

PARVEEN'S ANSWER

One physiological approach to stress management is to take drugs that are designed to lower the experience of stress and anxiety. These drugs include anti-anxiety drugs such as benzodiazepine (BZ) and beta-blockers. BZs work in the same way as neurotransmitters that usually slow down physical arousal in the body. BZs bind with the same receptors in the brain. Another way in which people can lower stress by using drugs is with beta-blockers. These drugs lower the level of sympathetic nervous system arousal in the body.

5/6

How to score full marks

Part (a)

🎯 MATTHEW'S ANSWER

Matthew's **definition of stress is completely circular** ('Stress means when you are stressed'), and a lay reader would be none the wiser about the nature of stress after reading this. It is clear from Matthew's later responses that he **does** understand the nature of stress, but this rather glib response is just a waste of two valuable marks, so 0/2. Matthew's **definition of a stressor is limited**, and makes no reference to the fact that a stressor is **a feature of the environment that produces a stress response** in the individual. He **does** point out that stressors produce stress, so there is understanding that they are the cause of a stress response, therefore he receives 1/2. Matthew's **definition of stress management deals with the essence of the term** so gets the full 2/2 marks.

🎯 PARVEEN'S ANSWER

Parveen does not make the mistake of simply recycling the term stress (stressed, stressor, etc.) but **explains** the term without having to rely on synonyms, so 2/2. Her **definition of a stressor is accurate** and focuses nicely on the two main aspects of this term as detailed above, so 2/2. Parveen's **definition of stress management is a model of a concise response** to this question. She refers to the **different ways** in which people **attempt to cope** with the **effects** of stress. This is suitably accurate and detailed, so 2/2.

Part (b)

🎯 MATTHEW'S ANSWER

Although Matthew has written a fair amount in his response to this question, **much of the content is vague or inappropriate**. The question clearly asks for a **description** of an approach to stress management, so **the evaluation of the use of drugs is clearly irrelevant in this context and would not receive any credit**. It is important in questions such as this to **focus your answer very directly on the specific requirements of the question** rather than simply filling your answer with material that may or may not be relevant. Matthew has correctly identified a physiological approach to stress management (the use of drugs), although his description of how such drugs reduce stress is extremely vague. Beta-blockers do more than simply 'altering the way that the brain works'.

🎯 PARVEEN'S ANSWER

Parveen has produced a **concise description** of how drugs might be used in stress management. This is an **appropriate approach** and Parveen has produced **an accurate account of the actions of selected anti-anxiety drugs**. There is not a lot more that would be required to gain full marks for this question. Parveen has described the action of BZs (they 'mimic' the actions of neurotransmitters that usually slow down physical arousal in the body). **Her description of the action of beta-blockers is more general and non-specific**. We are told that they 'lower the level of sympathetic nervous system arousal', but we are not told how they do this. **To gain full marks**, Parveen might have added that beta-blockers work by blocking receptors for the neurotransmitter noradrenaline (known as norepinephrine in the US), thus stopping it from activating the sympathetic nervous system.

Don't forget ...

- **Giving example**s in definitions can sometimes add that extra bit of detail to make sure of the full 2 marks.

- If asked to describe **one** approach, don't write about more than one unless they are all parts of the same broad 'approach'. For example, a number of different drugs might be taken to counter the effects of stress, but these all constitute the same basic approach – the use of drugs.

- **When asked for a description, provide some detail**. A definition or short sentence is not enough. Use the marks provided as a guide to how much you should write. Three minutes allows you to write a short paragraph, whereas for six minutes you should be writing twice as much.

- When asked to **describe** or **explain** something, don't waste time evaluating it, as this will not gain you extra marks.

- **When asked for two (or three) of something**, remember that each is marked independently, so don't spend too much time on one to the detriment of the other.

Matthew's answer to Question 1, part (c)

(c) To what extent are the effects of stress modified by gender differences? [18 marks]

> **The first part of this paragraph is appropriate AO1 descriptive content. Matthew has the date wrong here (it should be 1976) but doesn't lose any marks for this. It is good that he tries to *explain* why these gender differences might occur, as this counts as AO2 commentary.**

Women are thought to live longer than men because they are less physiologically aroused than men when in stressful situations (Frankenhauser et al., 1996). This might be because they make more use of social support networks or it may also mean that there are important physiological differences between men and women.

> **The answer is starting to slow down. It becomes obvious that Matthew has run out of things to say, so he is *recycling the same material* in slightly different forms – this adds very little.**

Men and women might differ in the way their nervous systems react to stressful situations. If men are more aroused by stressful situations this might explain why they don't tend to live as long as women do. Men don't make as much use of social networks and are more likely to keep things bottled up or turn to drink.

> **As suspected, Matthew has nothing more to say about gender differences. A speculative opening sentence is followed by material that has nothing to do with gender differences so earns *no more marks*.**

Men and women may also have different personalities. Research into personality differences has shown that some people display Type A behaviour, which is characterized by constantly working under time pressure and being more competitive than other people. There is a possibility that people with the Type A behaviour pattern are more likely to show signs of stress-related illness (such as coronary heart disease). This might affect one gender more than the other and so might explain why women tend to live longer than men.

AO1 = 2/6   AO2 = 2/12   Total = 4/18

Parveen's answer to Question 1, part (c)

(c) To what extent are the effects of stress modified by gender differences? [18 marks]

These first two sentences show clear AO1 description of gender differences.

Parveen shows awareness that there are *different* ways of interpreting the findings of this study (AO2).

The effects of stress are modified by gender in a number of ways. Stoney et al. (1990) found that women showed much smaller increases in blood pressure compared to men during stressful situations. This might indicate a physiological difference between men and women, with the stress pathways of women being less reactive than men, or alternatively, it may show that men and women differ in their attitude to stressful situations like examinations, with men being more competitive and therefore more aroused by competitive situations.

An interesting study. Parveen has presented a good précis of the Taylor et al. study (AO1) although she hasn't said how *males* deal with their stress.

Research by Taylor et al. (2000) has found that males and females respond differently to stress and that this might be the result of evolutionary differences between the sexes. They found that females tend to deal with their stress by seeking social contact and looking after their young, a process that they referred to as 'tending and befriending'.

A good explanation of *why* this difference exists. This lends some scientific credibility to the claims made earlier. As this is *commentary*, it counts as AO2 content.

Taylor et al. suggested that this 'tend and befriend' behaviour might be linked to the action of the hormone oxytocin, which is released at times of stress. This has been shown to make both animals and humans calmer and more social. Women appear to have more of this hormone and its action is amplified by the female hormone oestrogen. This would provide a physiological basis for gender differences in the way that males and females react to stress.

A good finale, with Parveen using another researcher's views to balance the claim that these differences are biologically determined. This is a very *effective use of the time available* so deserves full marks.

Taylor et al. (2000) argue that this gender difference may have evolutionary origins but Eagley (2000) disagrees, saying that different behaviours can be 'learned on the job', so we don't know how much of these gender differences are due to hormonal differences and how many are learned. It is possible that differences in the way that males and females deal with stress have nothing to do with biological factors but are simply a part of the gender-role socialization that males and females experience as they grow up.

18/18

How to score full marks for part (c)

🎯 Don't waste time

With 18 marks to earn in a relatively short period, it is important not to waste time. **Give only the information that is asked for**. Remember to **link all your points to the question clearly**, and always remember that both **AO1 and AO2** skills are required in this part of the question (see pages 8–11). You should structure your answer accordingly, paying due attention to the 6/12 split between AO1 and AO2 in this part of the question.

🎯 Stick to the question

It is **vitally important** in all the questions in this examination that you **stick rigidly to the exact question set**. Matthew does not do this – his exposition of personality differences in the experience of stress was not asked for, is not required and simply does not earn any credit. **It is better to write nothing at all and pass on to the next question than to waste time writing about something that is irrelevant**. Nor is it convincing to speculate, as Matthew does here, that there may be personality differences between the sexes that might account for the different ways in which males and females are affected by stressful situations. This may or may not be the case, but he has no **evidence** or **argument** to back up this suggestion, so really it isn't worth trying to make the link.

🎯 Use research evidence effectively

Parveen, on the other hand, **focuses on the question set at all times and constantly engages with the question in a critically searching way**. This is very effective, so we might spend a little time analysing why this was such a good response. First, she looks at claims for gender differences in the light of research evidence. Particularly when answering questions that begin with the instruction 'To what extent…', it is a good idea to **gather evidence** that might **support or challenge** the topic in question. Parveen does this, but Matthew simply makes assertions and does not attempt to back these up with research evidence.

🎯 Engage and elaborate

It is not sufficient merely to document gender differences in reactions to stress, but **effective critical commentary also requires you to engage with this material in a meaningful way**. Matthew offers a rather weak point that men may not live as long because 'they are more likely to keep things bottled up or turn to drink', but **fails to elaborate on this or support it at all**. This is a pity, because men **are** more prone to alcohol abuse as well as a number of other stress-related disorders, but we cannot assume that Matthew, from the information given here, knows about such research. Parveen, on the other hand, offers the suggestion that this may be due to the tendency for females to 'tend and befriend' in times of stress. Parveen also offers the fact that males and females differ in their levels of oxytocin, and that the action of this hormone is amplified by the female hormone oestrogen. It is not necessary to know about the actions of oxytocin, but the role suggested here for its action in stress reduction is perfectly reasonable, given the elaborate role played by this hormone in the brain.

🎯 Work logically towards a conclusion

Parveen also casts a critical eye over the claims that such differences between the sexes have a **biological** origin. Quoting the views of Alice Eagley, she suggests that differences in the ways that the sexes handle stress may be a product of **socialization** differences rather than biological factors, but it is difficult to disentangle the two. This is a good route through the answer. First, **look at the evidence for gender differences in the effects of stress**. Second, **try to explain the evidence**. Third, **be critical about the different explanations**. Although she does not say as much, it is fairly easy to conclude from Parveen's answer that the effects of stress **are** modified by gender differences, although the **reasons** for these differences cannot be certain.

Don't forget ...

- The **last part** of all AS questions (except for Research Methods) is **worth 18 marks** and so allow yourself adequate time to answer it well.

- This last part of the question will be assessing your **knowledge and understanding** of psychology (AO1 or Assessment Objective 1), and your ability to **analyse and evaluate** this material **in a clear and effective manner** (AO2 or Assessment Objective 2).

- **Two marks are allocated for the quality of written communication** shown in a paper. It is worthwhile trying to write clearly and accurately, using specialist terms correctly.

Stress

Stress may be seen as an aspect of the environment (the **stressor**) or the body's response to it (the **stress response**). Stress is more usually defined as a **deficit between the perceived demands of a situation and the perceived ability to cope** (the transactional model).

Stress as a bodily response

The body responds to stress in different ways. The main components of the stress response involve the **release of corticosteroids from the adrenal cortex and sympathetic arousal**, leading to increased secretion of adrenaline and noradrenaline from the adrenal medulla. The **General Adaptation Syndrome** was one of the first attempts to show how chronic stress could lead to illness. This has three stages, **alarm** (where the stress response is activated), **resistance** (as the body copes with stress) and **exhaustion** (where stress-related illness may develop). Stress can have **direct detrimental effects on health**, including the development of cardiovascular disorders, and **indirect effects** through the suppression of the immune system.

Sources of stress

Research has identified **life changes** (such as bereavement and divorce) as significant sources of stress, although more recent conceptualizations (such as the 'hassles' scale) have focused on the **minor stressors** of everyday life. The role of the workplace in the development of stress has emphasized a number of **organizational** sources of stress, which apply to most workers. These include relations with co-workers, workload, job insecurity and lack of control. Personality differences in the **reaction** to stress include Type A behaviour, which appears to make people more vulnerable to stress-related illness. Females appear to experience lower levels of stress-related arousal, which also makes them less vulnerable to stress-related illness.

Critical issue: Stress management

The potentially harmful effects of stress means that effective techniques for **stress management** are essential. Some techniques are **physiological** (such as the use of drugs), whilst others are **psychological** (such as meditation). Psychological approaches to stress can either be **general**, such as using relaxation techniques or meditation to reduce the body's state of arousal, or **specific**, using cognitive and behavioural training. **Meichenbaum's Stress-Inoculation training** has three phases (conceptualization, skills training and practice, real-life application). **Kobasa's notion of 'hardiness'** is taken to mean resistance to illness, or ability to deal with stress. Those who report the fewest illnesses show three kinds of hardiness (challenge, commitment and control).

The effectiveness of a particular technique is also determined by a range of other factors, including **previous experience, individual differences, social support** and **control**.

Question for you to try

Examiner's hints

- The first part of the question asks for **two** ways, therefore **divide your time equally** when answering this part.
- Take care that the procedures and conclusions you describe in part (b) are from the **same study**.
- Remember that in part (c) you need to provide 6 marks worth of AO1 and 12 marks worth of AO2, so divide your answer into **one-third AO1 and two-thirds AO2**.

Q2

(a) Outline **two** ways in which the body responds to stress. [3 marks + 3 marks]

(b) Describe the procedures and conclusions of **one** research study that has investigated the role of the workplace as a source of stress. [6 marks]

(c) Outline and evaluate **two or more** psychological approaches to stress management. [18 marks]

Answers are given on pp. 84–85.

Exam Questions

Time allowed: 30 minutes

Answer **one** question. You should attempt all parts of the question you choose.

Question 1

(a) Outline **two** attempts to define psychological abnormality.   [3 marks + 3 marks]

(b) Describe the procedures and findings from any **one** study that has investigated the causes of eating disorders.   [6 marks]

(c) 'Psychological abnormality can only be explained by considering a combination of psychological and biological factors.'

   To what extent does the biological (medical) model adequately account for the causes of psychological abnormality?   [18 marks]

Question 2

(a) Give **two** limitations of the 'statistical infrequency' definition of abnormality.   [3 marks + 3 marks]

(b) Outline the assumptions made by any **one** model of abnormality in relation to the causes of abnormality.   [6 marks]

(c) Consider the view that eating disorders can be explained in purely psychological terms.   [18 marks]

Take time to read both questions carefully, even though time is limited. **You will need to check what is in all parts of both questions before you can decide which question gives you the best opportunity to show what you know**. All the topic areas in the 'Individual Difference' section (i.e., 'Defining psychological abnormality', 'Biological and psychological models of abnormality' and 'Eating disorders') will be sampled across the two questions, but **this will not necessarily be the case within one question. You need to look carefully to see whether any topic area has been omitted** because this could be an important factor in making up your mind.

In this example, **both** questions sample **all** the topic areas, but the requirements of some of the questions are slightly different. Question 1 part (a), for example, asks you to outline **any two** attempts to define psychological abnormality, so you can choose the two you feel most confident about. Question 2 part (a), on the other hand, forces you to consider only the 'statistical infrequency' definition. However, **beware** of leaping into Question 1 because of this. You will need to look at parts (b) and (c) as well, before you decide which question to answer.

Think carefully about the specific wording of questions. Question 1 part (b), for example, requires a description of the procedures **and** findings from an eating disorder study. If you only know about the procedures, but can remember nothing about the findings of such a study, you will lose marks. In this case, it might better to consider Question 2 where you have a free choice of **any** of the models of abnormality on the specification.

It is very important to look at the last part of each question carefully. The last part is always worth 18 marks, and so part (c) should be a powerful factor in deciding between Question 1 or 2. This final part of the question requires you to use **AO2** skills as well as AO1, and so you are being asked to do **rather more here than simply describe the material**. There are 6 AO1 marks available in part (c), and so you will gain some credit for your ability to demonstrate knowledge and understanding of the issues. However, the majority of the marks (i.e.12 marks) are for AO2. **AO2 requires a rather different kind of skill** where you will have to show your ability to **analyse and evaluate** material and to offer **appropriate commentary**. You will need to think carefully about which of the two questions will allow you to demonstrate this skill to your best advantage. In this example, **both** questions require you to be able to consider causal explanations of abnormal disorders. However, in Question 2, you are tied to **a specific area of abnormal psychology** (i.e. eating disorders) whereas in Question 1, you can look **at a broader range of disorders** of your own choosing.

Laura and Luke decide to answer Question 1. Their answers are shown next.

(a) Outline **two** attempts to define psychological abnormality. [3 marks + 3 marks]

LAURA'S ANSWER

One way of defining abnormality is to say that people are failing to function properly. This is considered to be the most humane way of defining abnormality. Another way is when you deviate from social norms. Social norms are a bit like rules set down by society. If you do not follow these rules, you are abnormal. Rules are like not having babies outside marriage or being in a homosexual relationship, although some of these rules change over time.

⌐1/3⌐

⌐2/3⌐

LUKE'S ANSWER

One definition is the medical model, which is a biological approach. According to this, all psychological abnormality has a physical cause. Some mental disorders have a clear physical cause like alcohol poisoning or brain tumour but the cause of other disorders, like schizophrenia, has not yet been clearly identified.

Another definition is called deviation from mental health. This is where you are considered abnormal if you don't have all the characteristics of a mentally healthy person like being positive and able to adapt. However, this would be very difficult for most of us.

⌐0/3⌐

⌐2/3⌐

(b) Describe the procedures *and* findings from any **one** study that has investigated the causes of eating disorders. [6 marks]

LAURA'S ANSWER

Holland did a study on anorexia in twins. He found that the rate for identical twins was higher than the rate for non-identical twins. Another study was done on bulimia in twins and they also found the rate was higher for identical twins.

⌐1/6⌐

LUKE'S ANSWER

Fairburn et al. did a study on eating disorders. It was a very large study in which they compared people with eating disorders with other people. There were about 150 people in each group and they were all interviewed to find out things about their attitudes and their backgrounds. Fairburn found out certain things from the interview tapes. For example, people with eating disorders were perfectionist and they had low opinions of themselves.

(4/6)

How to score full marks

Part (a)

🎯 LAURA'S ANSWER

Laura has chosen two perfectly acceptable definitions of abnormality, but **she has not provided the appropriate level of detail in her outlines**. She has **identified** the 'failure to function adequately' definition, **but has really done little other than to name it**. The statement that it is a 'humane way of defining abnormality' is not **explained** and is, in any case, more of an evaluation than a description. This answer can only be awarded 1 mark. **For full marks, the answer needed to be more detailed and to explain exactly what is meant by a failure to function adequately**. It would have been useful to include an **example**, e.g. a depressed person who cannot sleep or concentrate and who has to take time off work.

Laura is a bit more successful with her second outline definition. She identifies the 'deviation from social norms' definition and explains what social norms are, giving appropriate, though dated, examples. She indicates that social norms differ over time, but **she does not make the point clearly that these changing norms affect judgements about abnormality**.

🎯 LUKE'S ANSWER

Luke has, unfortunately, misunderstood the requirements of the question. **This highlights the importance of knowing the specification and making sure that you understand the basic terminology**. Luke has described a **model of abnormality rather than a definition and so can earn no marks for his first answer**. He has, however, identified an appropriate definition (i.e., deviation from mental health) for his second answer and has outlined this reasonably accurately. **His last sentence contains an evaluation of the definition rather than an outline, and so gains no marks**. He would have used his time more profitably by naming some of the other criteria for mental health.

Part (b)

🎯 LAURA'S ANSWER

Laura has chosen an appropriate study but, unfortunately, **does not seem to have enough knowledge about it to answer the question adequately**. She mentions that the study was carried out on twins, which is a very weak and basic reference to procedure, and then provides a muddled sentence on the findings. For example, it is unclear what she means by 'the rate'. **She could have avoided this lack of clarity by simply adding the word 'concordance' before rate**.

It is sometimes difficult to give equal weighting to a description of the procedures and findings in a given study and you will find that this is not necessary. The important thing is that you include some description of both aspects. It is unlikely, for example, that you will know the exact details of how Holland et al. conducted their study, but you must include some reference to the basic procedure. Note that this could include the type of sample used. For example, you could write: 'Holland et al. conducted a study on sets of female twins who had been selected because one of the pair had been diagnosed with anorexia nervosa. Some of the twin pairs were monozygotic (MZ) and some were dizygotic (DZ). Holland et al. confirmed this relationship by using blood tests. They then investigated the other member of the twin pair to find out the concordance rate for anorexia.' **Note that the use of specialist terms** (e.g. *MZ* and *DZ twins* and the *concordance rate*) **allows you to express ideas succinctly**. You do **not** need to explain these specialist terms. As far as the findings are concerned, **it is useful if you can remember more detail** than Laura has provided. For example, in one study, Holland et al. found a concordance rate of 56 per cent in MZ twins compared with only 7 per cent in DZ twins. Moreover, in three cases where the twins did not have anorexia, there was evidence of her having another psychological disorder. Note that Holland and his colleagues conducted more than one study on the genetic basis of anorexia. **When you answer questions like these, you should make sure that you do not muddle the details of two separate studies**.

Laura has tried to pad out her answer by referring to a second study carried out to investigate the genetic basis of bulimia. **This is not a sensible strategy and Laura is simply wasting time**. The question requires a description of **one** study and **no credit will be given for a description of another one**. Her answer gains only 1 mark.

LUKE'S ANSWER

Luke has chosen a completely different kind of study and has been more successful in his description. **The question is broad-ranging and allows a wide choice of studies – any** study could be described, whether it concerns causal factors, incidence or treatment. Luke has accurately named the researcher who carried out this particular study and has correctly stated that the research was based on interviews. He has remembered that people with eating disorders were compared with other people, but **his description would have been more detailed if he had recalled the nature of the comparison groups**, i.e., one group of people with other kinds of psychological disorder and one group of mentally healthy people. He has not been quite accurate about the numbers in each group, although **the precise numbers would not be required for full marks**. He has accurately stated the findings, **although he has not made it explicitly clear** that the people with anorexia differed from the other groups. As it is, he earns 4/6 marks.

Don't forget ...

- Make sure that you **understand the terms used in the specification**. If you are asked for a **definition of abnormality, you will gain no marks if you describe a model**.

- **Look carefully at the mark allocation** at the end of each question part. There are **3 marks** for each outline of a definition in Question 1 part (a), but **6 marks** for the outline of the implications for treatment in part (b) of Question 2. Although an outline is required in both cases, **you would clearly need to include more detail** in the latter.

- If asked to give an outline, **do not waste time providing an evaluation as well**. You will gain no marks by doing this.

- If you are asked to describe the procedures **and** findings of a study, **you must choose one where you can accurately recall both these aspects of the study**.

- If you are asked to describe **one** study, **do not waste time** describing other studies. You will gain no marks for this.

Laura's answer to Question 1, part (c)

(c) 'Psychological abnormality can only be explained by considering a combination of psychological and biological factors.'

To what extent does the biological (medical) model adequately account for the causes of psychological abnormality? [18 marks]

Laura will gain some credit (AO1) for her description of the assumptions of the model, but she could have used some of this material *more effectively* to make an evaluative point as well, i.e. that the medical model can explain some disorders better than others.

The medical model sees psychological abnormality as a disease. For example, general paresis is known to be caused by syphilis. Other disorders like depression do not have a definite cause at the moment but the medical model thinks that a physical cause will be found. Physical causes can be genetic or to do with neurotransmitters in the brain or because of brain damage e.g. a head injury.

Phrases such as 'a good model' are *too vague*. Laura makes valid comments about 'no blame' and 'labelling', but fails to draw a *relevant* evaluative point.

It is a good model because it takes away blame from the individual. The person is seen as ill rather than evil. There is a problem that people get labelled with an illness e.g. schizophrenia.

Laura is hinting at a sound evaluative point here, i.e. that the medical model can account only for certain aspects of psychological abnormality, but, again, she does not make the *explicit* link to causal explanations.

The medical model uses drugs to treat mental illness. This can be good for people with depression because it may prevent suicide but it does not stop them being unhappy with their lives. They probably need counselling to help them as well.

People with schizophrenia have problems with certain neurotransmitters in the brain but this could be caused by the drugs and not by the illness.

This is a reasonable point – it refers to the difficulty of disentangling cause and effect – but, as before, the point is not made very *clearly*.

The medical model accounts for the causes of psychological disorders quite well but there are other models that give different points of view.

This is a weak concluding statement. Other models could be used effectively to evaluate the medical model, but Laura only hints at this.

AO1 = 4/6   AO2 = 5/12   Total = 9/18

Luke's answer to Question 1, part (c)

(c) 'Psychological abnormality can only be explained by considering a combination of psychological and biological factors.'

To what extent does the biological (medical) model adequately account for the causes of psychological abnormality? [18 marks]

Although the differences between psychiatrists and psychologists is not quite as clear-cut as this, Luke makes *relevant* commentary here about other possible causes of psychological abnormality. He addresses the question by stating that no single model offers an adequate explanation.

The biological model is the model usually preferred by doctors. They believe that mental illness is the same as physical illness. Many psychologists, on the other hand, think that psychological disorders are caused by factors such as the environment. It is probably true to say that biological and environmental factors both have a part to play. No model on its own can account for all types of psychological abnormality.

Another relevant point, *although it is not supported by evidence*. The role of media models in eating disorders could have been used as a good example here.

There are some psychological disorders where the physical cause seems clear. General paresis, for example, is caused by syphilis but researchers have not yet found the physical reason for some disorders. They are more likely to be caused by other things like stress or bad treatment as a child.

This is a related but separate point, i.e. that a single disorder might have more than one underlying cause.

It is also possible that a single disorder could be caused by different things and not just biological factors. Depression might be partly caused by faulty neurotransmitters in the brain but only in people who are also having bad life experiences.

There are *two* valid points here, but the commentary is *limited*.

If the medical model is right, then people with psychological disorders should get better with drugs. Some people get better but not everyone. Also sometimes the drugs themselves cause problems in the brain and it is difficult to know what came first.

Again, Luke makes a valid point but does not relate it *clearly* to the question. He then wastes time by repeating an idea already expressed. It is better to avoid phrases like: 'As I said before ...'

Genetics are important in the medical model and some disorders are thought to be passed on from parents. It is difficult to investigate this because families share the same environment as well as the same genes. As I said at the beginning of the essay, I think that psychological disorders are caused by a mixture of psychological and environmental factors.

AO1 = 4/6   AO2 = 8/12   Total = 12/18

How to score full marks for part (c)

Avoid irrelevant material

You only have approximately 18 minutes to answer this question so you **cannot afford to waste time on irrelevant material**. Laura, for example, has written an introductory paragraph that is poorly focused on the requirements of the question. She **describes the basic assumption** of the medical model and she gains some AO1 credit for this although the outline is pretty basic. However, she could have used the material much more effectively to **make an evaluative comment about the adequacy of the model**. She could, for example, have written something along the following lines: 'Research has demonstrated clearly that certain disorders e.g. general paresis have underlying physical causes, but it is not so clear-cut for other disorders like anorexia where behavioural or psychodynamic explanations may be more plausible.'

Relate evaluative points to the question

In her second paragraph, **Laura makes two evaluative points about the medical model but does not relate them to the question**, even though they could be made relevant. For example, by explaining psychological disorders in terms of illness, supporters of the medical model operate within a scientific framework, which encourages research. So, even though physical causes have not yet been found for all psychological disorders, it could be argued that research will eventually uncover them. On the other hand, the label of 'mental illness' can prevent people from looking for different, non-biological causes and so may give an unbalanced picture.

Make your evaluative points clear

Laura is slightly more focused in her next paragraph, **but she still does not make her evaluative point entirely clear**. The key point here is that biological treatments, e.g. drugs, have been shown to be effective in disorders such as depression. This lends weight to the idea that the underlying cause is also biological. However, drugs do not always work effectively and do not bring about a complete cure in people who are depressed. This suggests that other factors, such as life circumstances, might contribute to the origin of the disorder.

Use your material effectively

The last two paragraphs are similar in that they hint at evaluation without being explicit. She will gain some AO1 credit for describing relevant issues but she is not using AO2 skills appropriately. **This is such a pity because Laura has some good material throughout her answer, but she has not used it effectively to address the question**.

Use evidence to support your arguments

Luke has used very similar material in his answer, but he has managed to adapt it better to the requirements of the question. **The reason that he has not achieved higher AO2 marks is that his analysis is slightly limited and he has not always supported his arguments with evidence or examples**.

Consider strengths and weaknesses

In this type of question, **you need to consider both the strengths and the weaknesses of the model in order to be able to assess the extent to which it is effective**. However, **make sure that your evaluative comments are clearly linked to the question**. For example, it is a valid criticism of the model to say that it encourages people with psychological disorders to become passive and dependent. On its own, however, this statement does not help us to decide whether the model adequately accounts for the causes of psychological disorders and so would not gain any marks.

🎯 Use examples

It is unlikely that you will know about many specific studies in this area, but **it is important to try to support your arguments where possible**, e.g. by using examples. For example, Luke gained credit for his argument that certain disorders are better explained in psychological terms. **However, he would have made the point more powerfully if he had given anorexia nervosa as an example of such a disorder**. Similarly, he could have illustrated his point about genetic research by writing something like: 'Twin and family studies have provided support for the idea that certain disorders such as schizophrenia are transmitted genetically. However, social learning theorists would argue that family members often share the same environment as well as the same genes and might develop psychological disorders through modelling people around them.'

Don't forget ...

- The **last part** of all AS questions (except for Research Methods) is worth 18 marks. **Make sure that you allow yourself enough time to answer it in sufficient detail.**

- The last part of the question will assess your ability to **analyse and evaluate** theories, concepts, studies and methods and to **communicate** your knowledge and understanding of psychology in a **clear and effective manner** (AO2). You will not gain marks for simply describing models or research. Although there are 6 AO1 marks available, descriptive material must be relevant and, where possible, used only to introduce or elaborate an evaluative point.

- **Make your evaluative points clear and relevant**. Do not leave it up to the examiner to guess the point you are making – the examiner will not make the appropriate links for you.

- Remember that you need to **consider both sides of the argument** when you are asked to assess the extent to which a model/theory is supported. Not all part (c) questions will be introduced by a quotation but, where they are used, they are designed to help you. In this case, the quotation alerts you to the fact that you should consider psychological explanations as well as biological ones.

- **Two marks are allocated for the quality of written communication** on each paper. It is worthwhile trying to write clearly and accurately, using specialist terms correctly.

Abnormality

Abnormality is one topic within the area of individual differences. The term **psychological abnormality** refers to behaviours and psychological functioning which are considered to be different from normal. **There is no agreement as to the precise definition of the term abnormality and various suggestions have been put forward**.

Biological and psychological models of abnormality

Models of abnormality offer explanations about the origins of psychological disorders and also have implications for their treatment. According to the **biological (medical)** model, psychological disorders are illnesses caused by biological factors and should be treated with physical treatments, e.g. drugs. The **psychodynamic** model is a psychological model first developed by **Freud**, who believed that mental disorders arose from unresolved, unconscious conflicts experienced in childhood. The main goal of psychodynamic therapy is to enable individuals to access their repressed anxieties and conflicts and to resolve them. Another psychological model was put forward by the **behaviourists**. The basic assumption of this model is that all behaviour, including maladaptive or abnormal behaviour, is learned through processes such as classical and operant conditioning. Treatment involves further conditioning designed to remove the maladaptive behaviours. The central assumption of the **cognitive** model is that psychological disorders arise from irrational and distorted thinking patterns. Cognitive therapy aims to alter faulty thinking and replace it with more rational and positive beliefs.

Defining psychological abnormality

There have been many attempts to define the term 'psychological abnormality'. According to one definition, any behaviour that is **statistically infrequent** is seen as abnormal. A problem with this definition concerns the desirability of a particular behaviour or psychological ability. It is statistically rare to be classified as a genius, but this could be seen as a desirable quality and does not indicate clinical abnormality. The concept of **deviation from social norms** takes this factor into account and behaviour is judged to be abnormal if it contravenes accepted rules within a society. A rather different way of defining abnormality is in terms of **deviation from ideal mental health**. **Jahoda** identified a list of six characteristics which she believed defined mental health. An individual who does not demonstrate these characteristics is thought to be vulnerable to psychological problems. One limitation of this definition lies in the difficulty of measuring these characteristics. The fourth definition to be considered is the **failure to function adequately**. According to this approach, people behave abnormally when they fail to cope with everyday aspects of their life such as going to work or enjoying leisure time. **A major limitation of all the definitions is that they are culture-bound**. Behaviour that is acceptable to one group of people and at one period in history may be unacceptable to others.

Critical issue: eating disorders – anorexia nervosa and bulimia nervosa

The most common eating disorders are **anorexia nervosa** and **bulimia nervosa**. Anorexia is characterized by very low body weight, distorted body image and severely restricted food intake, whereas bulimia is characterized by episodes of secret binge eating followed by purging. Various explanations have been put forward to account for these disorders. **Biological explanations** include infection, hormonal imbalance and genetic transmission, but evidence for such factors is not strong. **Psychodynamic explanations** include avoidance of sexual maturity, sexual abuse and breakdowns in family dynamics. There is some support for such theories but research is limited. **Behaviourists** explain eating disorders in terms of **conditioning** and **modelling**. The fact that the incidence of eating disorders appears to differ across cultures lends some support to this view.

Question for you to try

Examiner's hints

- Make sure that you **clearly identify two** limitations in part (a). It is useful to start a new line when you give the second limitation so there is no uncertainty.
- You are required to give two limitations of **a specific definition** i.e. 'statistical infrequency'. **You will get no marks for identifying limitations of other definitions**.
- In part (b), you must outline the assumptions of causality according to **any one** model. You can choose any model so make sure that you pick one that you can write about in the most accurate detail.
- **Do not confuse the terms used in the specification**. In part (b), **you will get no marks if you write about definitions rather than models**.
- In part (b), **you are only being asked for an outline. Do not waste time giving an evaluation**.
- Remember that in part (c), the majority of the marks (i.e. 12) are awarded for AO2 skills. In other words, you will need to show your **skills in analysing and evaluating** psychological explanations of eating disorders. You will not get full marks simply by describing explanations of eating disorders.

Q2

(a) Give **two** limitations of the 'statistical infrequency' definition of abnormality.

[3 marks + 3 marks]

(b) Outline the assumptions made by any **one** model of abnormality in relation to the causes of abnormality. [6 marks]

(c) Consider the view that eating disorders can be explained in purely psychological terms. [18 marks]

Answers are given on pp. 86–87.

Exam Questions

Time allowed: 30 minutes

Answer **one** question. You should attempt all parts of the question you choose.

Question 1

(a) Outline findings of research into majority social influence (conformity).

[6 marks]

(b) Describe the findings *and* conclusions of **one** study of obedience.   [6 marks]

(c) Discuss how psychologists have dealt with the ethical issues raised by research into social influence.   [18 marks]

Question 2

(a) Explain what is meant by the terms 'social influence', 'minority influence' and 'obedience'.   [2 marks + 2 marks + 2 marks]

(b) Outline **two** explanations of why people yield to minority influence.

[3 marks + 3 marks]

(c) To what extent are the ethical objections levelled against social influence research, such as that carried out by Milgram and Zimbardo, justified?

[18 marks]

Be sure to read both questions carefully before you start writing. In this way you will select the question that will enable you to score the highest marks. **Do a rough calculation to work out how many marks in each question you think you can achieve**. Don't just make up your mind on the basis of the first couple of parts in each question. Which of the questions on page 55 would you choose?

Although all topic areas in 'Social Influence' will be sampled over the two questions, this will not necessarily occur within any one question. **Take care not to rush into answering a question just because the first couple of parts are about an area you particularly enjoyed**. Later parts may ask you about another area altogether. Question 1, for example, begins with a question on conformity, but part (b) deals with obedience and part (c) concerns ethical issues. Of course, sometimes a question will deal with only one or two topics.

Whether or not you have preferences for individual topics, you will still need to **read each part of the two questions carefully and note their specific requirements**. In Question 1, for example, part (b) asks you to describe the findings **and** conclusions from one study of obedience. If you know only about the findings but nothing about the conclusions of studies in this area, you will lose marks. You might be better off answering Question 2 provided you can outline **two** explanations of why people yield to minority influence.

It is **important to look at part (c)** of each question before choosing which to answer because this part of a question is worth more marks than the other two parts combined. Remember that **part (c) of a question (worth 18 marks) requires both AO1 and AO2 skills**. That is, you are asked to do more than just describe material relevant to the area. You are also asked to **engage** with the material in a specific way. In Question 1 you are asked to 'discuss…', which requires you to **describe and evaluate** how psychologists have dealt with the ethical issues raised by research into social influence. Note that **6 marks are available for AO1 content** (e.g. describing how psychologists have tried to deal with ethical issues) and **12 marks are available for AO2 content** (e.g. evaluating how successful psychologists have been in dealing with ethical issues). Therefore, although some AO1 content is required it is how you engage with it that will determine how many AO2 marks you earn. Question 2 asks 'to what extent…', which requires you to **weigh up the evidence** that ethical objections levelled against social influence research are justified. Again there are 6 marks available for AO1 content (e.g. describing the ethical objections) and 12 marks for AO2 content (e.g. critically reviewing the arguments that these objections are justifiable). Note that although both questions deal with ethical issues, each question has a different focus:

Question 1 focus: Discussing **attempts to deal with** ethical issues.

Question 2 focus: Judging whether **ethical objections** to social influence research are **justified**.

Sarah and Sam decide to answer Question 1. Their answers are shown next.

(a) Outline findings of research into majority social influence (conformity).

[6 marks]

SARAH'S ANSWER

Asch asked participants to compare the length of a line with three other lines. Participants came to a laboratory and sat in a semi-circle. They were shown a card with a line on it and then another card with 3 lines. They were asked to call out loud which one of the 3 lines was the same as the first line. There were accomplices who called out the wrong answer on certain trials. Then the real participant called out his answer. 74% of participants gave the wrong answer at least once. Asch changed the procedures and found that the levels of conformity changed. If the accomplices were not unanimous the participants conformed less. This study has been criticised because it lacks ecological validity and is not like real life.

2/6

SAM'S ANSWER

Majority social influence was investigated by Asch. He found that when a majority of 6 accomplices exerted unanimous pressure on one participant to give a wrong answer to an easy question about line lengths that participants conformed on 32% of trials. 74% of participants conformed at least once. If the majority was not unanimous in giving the same wrong answer, conformity levels dropped to 5%. Other factors that reduced levels of conformity were having a majority of only two and allowing participants to write their answers rather than call them out. These findings have been supported by other researchers but later in Britain, almost no conformity was found by Perrin and Spencer. Zimbardo also found that people would conform to new social roles in a prison simulation study.

4/6

(b) Describe the findings *and* conclusions of **one** study of obedience. [6 marks]

SARAH'S ANSWER

Milgram invited volunteers to come to his lab to take part in an experiment about learning and memory. When the men arrived at the lab they sat at a shock generator and gave shocks to another man when he gave wrong answers. Most volunteers gave shocks up to 450 volts even though the 'learner' screamed to be let out and even stopped answering altogether. Women also gave shocks when told to do so. The conclusions from this study are that people will give shocks to other people if someone in authority tells them to.

3/6

SAM'S ANSWER

In one study of obedience a doctor phoned and asked a nurse to give a drug to a patient before he arrived. This broke hospital rules. Most nurses began to give the drug (a harmless substance really) until they were stopped by another nurse. The conclusion from this study is that nurses cannot be trusted and will do whatever doctors ask them to. In another study looking at obedience in nurses it was found that most of them disobeyed. Therefore sometimes nurses can be trusted.

2/6

How to score full marks

Part (a)

🎯 SARAH'S ANSWER

Sarah's answer gains only 2/6 because it is **basic** and **lacking detail**. She provides only one detailed finding from Asch's research (that 74% of participants conformed at least once). She correctly points out that when the majority is not unanimous that participants conformed less. However, there is no detail and she does not say how far the level fell. Sarah's answer falls into two traps. The question asked **only** for **findings** and so no credit is given for the procedural detail at the beginning or the evaluative comment at the end of the answer.

🎯 SAM'S ANSWER

Sam's answer gains 4/6 because it is **generally accurate** and provides some **detail**. He avoids getting bogged down in accounts of procedures and does not waste time giving evaluations. He gives three detailed results from Asch's studies and summarises some other findings. He does not do justice, however, to Perrin and Spencer's findings which were more complex than he suggests and the findings of Zimbardo's study need to be described in more detail.

Part (b)

🎯 SARAH'S ANSWER

Sarah wastes time describing (not entirely accurately) Milgram's procedures. First, you should describe the **findings** of the study (e.g. 65 per cent of participants 'gave shocks' up to 450 volts; no one stopped before 300 volts; under which conditions obedience rates increased and decreased). Next you should describe the **conclusions** (e.g. situational factors are largely responsible for obedience; the majority of ordinary people will obey even when this goes against conscience). **Note that Sarah gives only one conclusion, when the question requires at least two**.

🎯 SAM'S ANSWER

Sam has given the correct finding from Hofling's obedience study, but once again he needs to provide more detail (e.g. the exact percentage of nurses who obeyed; that all the telephone conversations with the 'doctor' were short; that nurses reported often being asked to break hospital rules). Neither of the conclusions given is valid, going well beyond what can be concluded from one limited study. You could conclude that in 1966 nurses were inclined to obey a medical authority figure rather too readily and that obedience can be demonstrated in real-life situations as well as in a laboratory. **Note that Sam's reference to 'another study' gains no marks, as only one study was required by the question**.

Don't forget ...

- If asked to describe **more than one** explanation or process etc., be sure to do so. Try to do each in appropriate detail, as each will be marked independently.
- If asked for information about **one** study, write about only one study!
- **When asked for an outline or a description etc., provide some detail**. A definition or short sentence is not enough. However, remember that you have only got three minutes approximately for a 3-mark answer.

- When choosing a study to describe, take care to select one about which you know enough of the **right sort of detail**.
- **Look out for plurals** in a question, such as finding**s** or conclusion**s**.

Sarah's answer to Question 1, part (c)

(c) Discuss how psychologists have dealt with the ethical issues raised by research into social influence. [18 marks]

> **What is meant by the term 'ethical'? Wastes time asking a question which cannot be answered. Chatty style is inappropriate.**

Psychologists have to be careful to carry out their research in an ethical way. How would you like to be tricked into giving shocks to someone and maybe thinking you'd killed them?

> **Getting there – three ethical issues mentioned: protection from harm; deception; right of withdrawal.**

Milgram and Zimbardo have been criticized for not taking enough care of their participants. Milgram did not tell them the truth. He deceived them so they thought they were taking part in a study about memory. He insisted they carry on giving shocks even when they wanted to stop.

> **Good, Sarah mentions use of guidelines to deal with ethical issues (AO1 content) _but no evaluation or commentary offered._ Content of guidelines is not entirely accurate.**

Psychologists use guidelines today that stop them deceiving participants. They also have to let participants leave any time they want.

> **Oh dear, Sarah is wasting time describing Zimbardo's study without explicitly linking the ethical issues that arise here with psychologists' attempts to deal with them. _Still no evaluation._**

In Zimbardo's prison study he had some students arrested at their homes without warning and kept as prisoners. Other students acted as their guards to keep them under control. They began to abuse the prisoners. One prisoner broke down and had to be let out. This is not ethical. You cannot keep people locked up in psychology experiments nowadays.

> **In total, four ethical guidelines listed (AO1 content) but _no detail or evaluation given._ Sarah needs to explain the relevance of countries having different guidelines if this is to earn AO2 marks.**

Psychology guidelines say you have to tell participants the truth, debrief them, get their consent and protect them. If psychologists do this, their research will be ethical. Different countries have different guidelines.

AO1 = 3/6   AO2 = 3/12   Total = 6/18

Sam's answer to Question 1, part (c)

(c) Discuss how psychologists have dealt with the ethical issues raised by research into social influence.　　　　　　　　　　　　　　　　　　[18 marks]

Good start, but Sam needs to *explain* term 'ethical issues'.

Ethical issue of deception identified. Lack of *fully* informed consent hinted at, but not made explicit.

The research of social psychologists such as Milgram and Zimbardo and Asch raised several ethical issues. Milgram and Asch deceived their participants about the real purpose of their research. Zimbardo's participants knew they had volunteered for a prison simulation study but they did not know whether they would be guards or prisoners.

Sam gets to grips with how psychologists have tried to deal with issue of deception.
Credit given for both AO1 and AO2 content. Good evaluative point.

Since these studies, psychologists have developed sets of guidelines to prevent participants being deceived unless it is really necessary. One way to avoid deceiving people is to tell them everything about the study and ask them to role-play as if they had not been told. Generally, however, using role-play gives results different from those found when participants are naive. So this attempt to deal with deception is not altogether successful.

Still on deception. Sam knows a lot about this but should be moving on to another issue. However, AO1 content is credited.

Another way to get around deceiving participants is to use only those people who previously have said that they do not mind being deceived. This is called prior general consent.

Presumably running out of time, Sam briefly mentions other ethical issues covered in the guidelines (AO1 content) and *makes one evaluative point but not very clearly.* He would make a better point by adding that this is a powerful incentive for psychologists to adhere to the guidelines.

BPS guidelines say that participants should be protected from harm, should give fully informed consent before a procedure starts and be debriefed at the end. Psychologists who ignore the guidelines can be expelled from the BPS.

AO1 = 4/6　　AO2 = 5/12　　Total = 9/18

Answer the question set

With 18 marks to earn in a short period, it is important not to waste time. **Give only the information that is asked for**. Where possible, use **psychological terminology**. This will enable you to write succinctly and help you to **communicate in a clear and effective manner**. Remember to **link all your points to the question clearly** and bear in mind that both AO1 and AO2 skills are required in this part of the question. Therefore, structure your answer so that it reflects the 6/12 split between AO1 and AO2 marks for this part of the question.

Avoid rhetorical questions

Avoid asking the examiner questions (as Sarah did). Your job is to answer questions, not ask them! You are asked to '**discuss** how psychologists have dealt with ethical issues'. This means you are required to **describe and evaluate** how ethical issues have been dealt with by psychologists.

Identify key ethical issues

First, explain what you mean by an 'ethical issue', i.e. a concern about what is considered right or acceptable. Quickly **identify** some of the issues thrown up by social influence research, e.g. whether deception can ever be justified, the need for informed consent and the protection of participants.

How psychologists deal with ethical issues

Next, look at how psychologists have tried to deal with these, e.g. by developing guidelines, setting up ethical committees and by using different research methods such as role-playing. Mention these so that it is clear what you are discussing. However, **do not spend too long describing them**. Your answer needs to be properly balanced and only 6 marks are given for AO1 content.

How to earn AO2 marks

To earn AO2 marks you could consider to what extent you think the BPS ethical guidelines provide adequate safeguards. For example, if psychologists infringe the code they may well be expelled from the BPS. You might also consider **what factors could affect the effectiveness of the ethics committees** who make decisions about the suitability of research projects. The **composition** of ethics committees (whether they contain lay members) and **how rigorously they operate** are important factors. Some people argue that dependence on centralised sets of rules removes responsibility from individual researchers who may conduct inferior research just because an ethics committee did not stop it. **Codes of conduct and ethical guidelines, therefore, do not guarantee high ethical standards**. Standards are influenced also by those who are on the committees and by how rigorously the guidelines are enforced.

Note also that all A level psychology students carry out a research study, very few of which will be scrutinised by an ethics committee. You might also note that at any given time **different countries are using different sets of guidelines**. Furthermore, guidelines are revised regularly in order to reflect changes in society's views and so no single set of guidelines provides a universal or absolute truth about what is the right way to conduct research.

Other ways to score full marks ...

In addition (or as an alternative) to discussing the effectiveness of guidelines and ethical committees, **you could also discuss some of the problems of trying to adhere to guidelines while still carrying out research that is meaningful and valuable**. The use of role-play, for example, as an alternative to deception does not usually produce the same results as those found by Asch and Milgram. **You could also consider the problems of trying to weigh up the relative cost of doing research** (e.g. potential harm to participants) **against the potential benefits to society**. As you can see, there is more than one way of providing a thorough and effective answer to this question.

Don't forget ...

- The **last part** of all AS questions (except for 'Research Methods') is **worth 18 marks**, so allow yourself adequate time to answer it well.

- This last part of the question will be assessing your **knowledge and understanding** of psychology (AO1 or Assessment Objective 1) and your ability to **analyse and evaluate** this material **in a clear and effective manner** (AO2 or Assessment Objective 2).

- **Two marks are allocated for the quality of written communication** shown in a paper. It is worthwhile trying to write clearly and accurately, using specialist terms correctly.

Key points to remember

Social influence
Social influence refers to the way in which other people affect a person's **attitudes** and **behaviour**. There are different types of social influence, including **majority** and **minority** as well as **obedience** to an authority figure.

Conformity and minority influence
The term 'conformity' refers to yielding (submitting) to the views of a majority. Research studies have shown how individuals can be influenced to conform to the views of majority groups (e.g. **Asch**) and to social norms (e.g. **Zimbardo**). **Minority social influence** occurs when a smaller group (or an individual) persuades a larger group to change its attitudes or behaviours. Minority influence may operate by means of converting majorities so that the effects, though slower to show, are more long-lasting than the effects of **majority influence**, where people may conform in public but not change their views in private.

Obedience to authority
Obedience refers to **complying with the requests or orders of someone in authority**. Many research studies have shown how readily people obey authority figures. **Milgram** carried out the first studies in obedience and his research has been accused of lacking validity. However, his studies have been replicated in other situations (e.g. **Hofling**) and in other countries (e.g. **Meeus and Raaijmakers**). The reasons proposed for people obeying include: gradual commitment; lapsing into an agentic state so that one no longer feels responsible for one's own actions; not wanting to cause a fuss by disobeying; having an authoritarian personality and therefore submitting to those in authority. People may **resist** pressures to obey if they retain a sense of personal responsibility, possess high levels of moral reasoning, see other people disobey or feel that they are being pressured too blatantly.

Critical issue: Ethical issues in psychological research
Ethical issues that concern research psychologists include the use of **deception**, obtaining **fully informed consent**, ensuring participants know they are **free to leave at any time** during the procedure and **protecting participants from harm**. Many ethical criticisms have been levelled against research in the area of social influence (particularly against Milgram's work), but some psychologists believe the importance of the issues researched outweighs the risk of harm to participants. Psychologists have developed **ethical guidelines** to provide a moral framework within which research is conducted. These guidelines are regularly revised to reflect changing social values.

Question for you to try

Q2

(a) Explain what is meant by the terms 'social influence', 'minority influence' and 'obedience'.   [2 marks + 2 marks + 2 marks]

(b) Outline **two** explanations of why people yield to minority influence.
[3 marks + 3 marks]

(c) To what extent are the ethical objections levelled against social influence research, such as that carried out by Milgram and Zimbardo, justified?
[18 marks]

Answers are given on pp. 88–89.

Exam Question

Time allowed: 30 minutes

You should attempt all parts of the question.

Question

In an attempt to test the anxiety-reducing properties of a new anti-anxiety drug *sedinex*, doctors prescribed the drug to 12 patients referred for job-related stress symptoms. A control group of 12 patients was prescribed a placebo (a pill that has no physiological effect) instead of *sedinex*. Participants were not aware that they were taking part in a clinical trial of the drug.

A number of physiological measurements were taken before treatment and after patients had been on their respective treatments for one week. Patients were also asked to keep a diary and rate how stressed they felt at the end of each working day (on a scale of 1 [not at all stressed] to 10 [extremely stressed]). Results for resting heart rate and subjective stress rating (how stressed the participants felt) are summarized in the graphs below.

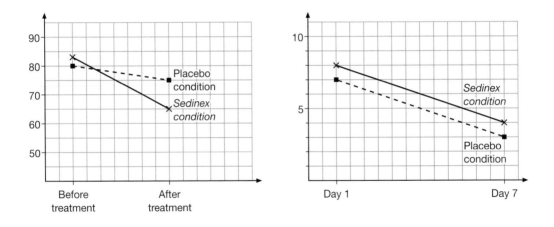

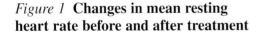
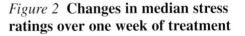

Figure 1 **Changes in mean resting heart rate before and after treatment**

Figure 2 **Changes in median stress ratings over one week of treatment**

(a) Suggest a suitable directional (one-tailed) hypothesis for this investigation.

[2 marks]

(b) Explain what is meant by an independent variable (IV). [2 marks]

(c) Identify the independent variable used in this investigation. [1 mark]

(d) Explain why it was considered necessary to use a control group that received only the placebo instead of *sedinex*. [2 marks]

(e) Why was it important for participants to keep a diary of their subjective stress ratings during the study? [2 marks]

(f) Identify **one** possible source of investigator effect in this study, and explain how you might attempt to overcome it. [3 marks]

(g) Using the information in Figure 1 and Figure 2, give **two** conclusions about the effectiveness of sedinex as an anti-anxiety drug. [2 marks + 2 marks]

(h) Describe **two** ethical issues that might have arisen in this investigation. [2 marks + 2 marks]

(i) Explain how the researchers might have dealt with the ethical issues described in part **(f)**. [2 marks + 2 marks]

(j) Explain **two** ways in which the design of this study might affect the validity of the results. [3 marks + 3 marks]

Students' answers to Question, parts (a) to (c)

(a) Suggest a suitable directional (one-tailed) hypothesis for this investigation. [2 marks]

HELENA'S ANSWER

The effect of sedinex will be greater than the effect of the placebo.

1/2

CHRIS'S ANSWER

Participants who take sedinex show less signs of anxiety after a week than those who take a placebo.

2/2

(b) Explain what is meant by an independent variable (IV). [2 marks]

HELENA'S ANSWER

Something that is independent of all the other variables in the experiment, i.e. not affected by them.

0/2

CHRIS'S ANSWER

An independent variable is something that an experimenter manipulates in an experiment so that they can measure its effect on the dependent variable.

2/2

(c) Identify the independent variable used in this investigation. [1 mark]

HELENA'S ANSWER

The drug condition (sedinex or placebo).

1/1

CHRIS'S ANSWER

It is something that is manipulated by the researcher to see its effect on something else.

0/1

How to score full marks

Part (a)

HELENA'S ANSWER

Helena's hypothesis does contain some of the essential ingredients for a directional hypothesis – it predicts a **causal relationship** between *sedinex* and, presumably, the amount of subsequent anxiety, and this is indeed stated **directionally**. However, **this is far too vague, and we are left filling in some of the details on Helena's behalf**. What **sort** of effect is being predicted here, and how would we know how to measure it? In technical terms, **Helena has failed to operationalize her dependent variable**. She should have specified the exact effect that *sedinex* would have (in this case, she might have said that it would lower heart rate, or make people feel less stressed). **Although she is on the right track with this hypothesis, it is too vague for the full 2 marks**.

CHRIS'S ANSWER

Chris's hypothesis is much better. He has predicted a **causal** relationship between *sedinex* and signs of anxiety, and has stated that the experimental group will show fewer signs of anxiety (this is what makes it **directional**) than the control group (thus comparing the two conditions in the study). **By adding that this effect will be evident at the end of a week, he has also made it clear that he expects an experimental effect** as a result of taking the *sedinex*, and not one as a result of taking the placebo. His answer therefore scores the full 2 marks.

Part (b)

HELENA'S ANSWER

Helena is clearly confused here as she offers little more than a guess in response to this question. Despite the fact she knows what the IV is in this study (see her next answer), she cannot offer a suitable definition. **Guessing can sometimes pay off**, but not in this case.

CHRIS'S ANSWER

Chris has offered an accurate **and detailed definition of an independent variable that includes two important characteristics** – 'that an experimenter manipulates…' and '…can measure its effect on the dependent variable'. **This is a good definition and is clearly worth full marks**.

Part (c)

HELENA'S ANSWER

Helena has correctly identified the independent variable as the drug condition that participants were placed in. She has elaborated on this by adding (in brackets) that she means the 'sedinex or placebo' conditions. **This is a good thing to do as it ensures full marks**.

CHRIS'S ANSWER

Chris appears to have misunderstood the requirements of the question. He has again **defined what an independent variable is rather than**, as asked for in the question, **what it is in this investigation**.

(d) Explain why it was considered necessary to use a control group that received only the placebo instead of *sedinex*. [2 marks]

HELENA'S ANSWER

It was necessary to use a control group that didn't receive sedinex because otherwise the researchers wouldn't know what had had the effect.

1/2

CHRIS'S ANSWER

The placebo condition helped the researchers to discount any effects that might have been due to participants simply believing that they were taking an anti-anxiety drug. If the drug really did have an effect, it should be greater than the effect shown by the placebo alone.

2/2

(e) Why was it important for participants to keep a diary of their subjective stress ratings during the study? [2 marks]

HELENA'S ANSWER

So the participants could keep a record of whether they felt differently over the week, as stress is all about what we feel as much as whether our body acts differently.

2/2

CHRIS'S ANSWER

Participants were asked to keep a record of their subjective stress ratings so these could be compared to the actual changes in resting heart rate over the same period. It is useful to have this extra information as change in heart rate alone may not be a reliable indicator of changes in stress levels.

2/2

(f) Identify **one** possible source of investigator effect in this study, and explain how you might attempt to overcome it. [3 marks]

HELENA'S ANSWER

The researchers may treat the participants in each group differently and this may affect their response to the drug. They should treat them the same so that this wouldn't affect the way they responded to the drug (or the placebo).

1/3

CHRIS'S ANSWER

It is possible that the investigators prescribed the sedinex to participants who originally showed greater stress-related symptoms. One way to overcome this would be to use a double blind procedure so that the doctors prescribing the drugs were not aware of the severity of the participants' symptoms (e.g. their blood pressure) at the start of the study.

(3/3)

How to score full marks

Part (d)

HELENA'S ANSWER

Helena has provided an answer which is along the right lines. She is aware that a control group is there as a way of seeing whether the drug had an effect. There is a fair amount of 'assisted reading' going on here on Helena's behalf. What exactly does she mean by the phrase 'wouldn't know what had had the effect'? **It would have helped Helena if she could simply have added something along the lines of Chris's second sentence**. As it is, she scores only 1 mark. It is often frustrating for the examiner to find that students know a lot more, but simply fail to add this to their answer when they obviously have time to do so. It doesn't matter if your language is not as precise as Chris's, but **you should try to illuminate your answer with something that makes the meaning of your statement as clear as possible**.

CHRIS'S ANSWER

Chris has done exactly that by explaining why a placebo condition was being used (to discount any effects due to participants believing they were receiving treatment) **and explaining how this would work in practice**. He tells us, quite rightly, that if the drug really did work, it should have more of an effect than the placebo alone. **This is a very effective answer so deserves both of the marks available**.

Part (e)

HELENA'S ANSWER

Helena is aware that the gathering of stress ratings is important because they **add an extra dimension to the measurement of stress**. She qualifies this by stating that 'stress is all about what we feel as much as whether our body acts differently'. **This is a sensible addition and guarantees the full two marks for this part of the question**. Although Helena would not lose any marks for the content in this answer, **she needs to write in complete sentences to make sure she does not lose any of the marks awarded for Quality of Written Communication (QoWC)**.

CHRIS'S ANSWER

Chris has also seen the importance of gathering this extra bit of information during the study. **He is aware that subjective stress ratings could usefully be compared to the changes in resting heart rate** and qualifies this by explaining that heart rate may not be a **reliable** indicator of stress levels by itself. **Note that Chris has written in complete sentences so does not put his QoWC marks under threat**.

Part (f)

🎯 HELENA'S ANSWER

Helena has suggested that the participants in each group might be treated differently by the researchers. Although she doesn't expand on this (i.e. treated differently in what ways?), this is sufficient as an **identification** of an investigator effect in this study. However, she then **simply repeats this problem without really offering any concrete suggestions how to overcome it**, so receives no marks for the resolution of this problem.

🎯 CHRIS'S ANSWER

Chris has likewise highlighted the problem of differential treatment, but has also **included a clear and detailed account** of how a double blind procedure might be used to overcome this. Note that Chris has **made sure of the full marks available** by elaborating this latter part of his answer. This is essentially a 1 + 2 mark question and Chris has balanced his answer accordingly.

Students' answers to Question, parts (g) to (i)

(g) Using the information in Figure 1 and Figure 2, give **two** conclusions about the effectiveness of *sedinex* as an anti-anxiety drug. [2 marks + 2 marks]

HELENA'S ANSWER

The group that takes sedinex does better after a week than the group that takes the placebo, (1/2)

but there isn't a lot of difference between the two groups in Figure 2. (1/2)

CHRIS'S ANSWER

Figure 1 shows that the mean resting heart rate of the participants who have been taking sedinex drops significantly over the week's trial compared to the placebo condition. (2/2)

Participants in the sedinex condition <u>and</u> those in the placebo condition feel less stressed after the week and there isn't a lot of difference in the levels of subjective stress ratings between the two groups. (2/2)

(h) Describe **two** ethical issues that might have arisen in this investigation. [2 marks + 2 marks]

HELENA'S ANSWER

It is not ethical to withhold treatment (such as anti-anxiety drugs) from people who have need for them. This is wrong because it puts them at risk. (2/2)

Also it is wrong to deceive people in the placebo condition into thinking that they are taking a drug that will make them better when in fact they aren't. This may result in them relying on the drug and taking no other steps to reduce their stress symptoms. ②/2

CHRIS'S ANSWER

Participants were not given the opportunity to give their informed consent to take part in this study. Informed consent means having enough information to make a reasoned decision about taking part in a study. ①/2

The participants who were put on the placebo were not given the appropriate medication to deal with their stress-related symptoms. This is unethical because it does not protect them from physical harm. ②/2

(i) Explain how the researchers might have dealt with the ethical issues described in part (f).

[2 marks + 2 marks]

HELENA'S ANSWER

The researchers might have put the placebo group on a different anti-anxiety drug such as valium. ①/2

They should have told all participants what they were letting themselves in for. This may have influenced the results of the study, but the health of the participants is more important, and they need to understand all the potential risks. ②/2

CHRIS'S ANSWER

All participants should have been given sufficient information about the potential risks of participation to have been able to give their informed consent whether or not to take part. ②/2

In order to protect those in the placebo condition, participants should have been checked regularly throughout the study. They might, for example, have worn blood pressure monitors which were checked regularly by a doctor. ②/2

How to score full marks

Part (g)

HELENA'S ANSWER

Helena has correctly interpreted the two graphs, but her interpretation is rather imprecise and lacking in detail. Figure 1 shows a fall in the resting heart rate of both groups, but this is more pronounced in the *sedinex* group than in the placebo group. **It isn't sufficient simply to say that one group 'does better' than the other, because 'better' isn't defined.** Likewise, for her second conclusion, Helena points out that there 'isn't a lot of difference' between the two groups, but doesn't explain in what way there isn't a difference. **She should have pointed out that there was little difference in terms of change in resting heart rate over the duration of the study.** It may seem obvious to you what you are talking about when using such imprecise phrases, but **the exact relationship should always be spelt out for maximum marks**. As it is, Helena's answer scores only 2 out of the possible 4 marks.

CHRIS'S ANSWER

Chris correctly points out that the mean resting heart rate 'drops significantly' over the week's trial 'compared' to the placebo condition. **Note that Chris's answer is far more precise. He states exactly what change is indicated in Figure 1** (i.e., change in the mean resting heart rate) and demonstrates this comparatively by stating the difference between the two conditions in this respect. **Chris's second conclusion takes account of the information in Figure 2 and again states the precise change** (in subjective stress ratings) over the week. This time he concludes that 'there isn't a lot of difference in the levels of subjective stress ratings between the two groups'. His answer deserves the full 4 marks.

Part (h)

HELENA'S ANSWER

Helena has clearly got her teeth into this question. **She is aware that the withholding of treatment from people who may need it is ethically unacceptable.** She qualifies this by suggesting that this may put them at risk. This is fine for the **full two marks**.

Her second ethical issue relates the cost of deception to potential harm for the participant. **This is a clever point, and sufficiently detailed for full marks**.

CHRIS'S ANSWER

Chris has suggested that participants may not have given their **informed consent** to take part in the study and goes on to explain what is meant by informed consent. **This is quite appropriate**, as we are told that the **participants were not aware that they were taking part in a clinical trial of the drug**, therefore, presumably, were not able to give their full **informed** consent. This is a difficult question to mark as the question does ask for an ethical issue that **might** arise. However, **it is always better to go for less speculative ethical issues that are more obviously part of the study being described**.

Chris's second ethical issue is much clearer. The placebo group participants clearly were **not** given the appropriate medication which, as Chris points out, might expose them to physical harm. Unlike his first point, this is **less speculative**.

Part (i)

HELENA'S ANSWER

There is some value in this suggestion, particularly **if the effects of the alternative drug are well documented**. Examiners would not assume that students fully understand how a drug 1 versus drug 2 clinical trial works unless this is made explicit in the answer. Helena's suggestion does alter the nature of the study in such a way that it would make it more difficult to test the merits of *sedinex* against a control of no treatment at all.

In response to the second ethical issue, Helena **has suggested full disclosure of all**

procedures. She is, of course, quite right about the primacy of participant care over methodological concerns, so **this is an appropriate suggestion worthy of full marks**.

CHRIS'S ANSWER

Chris has suggested that all participants are given 'sufficient' information about the risks of participation. Note that he is realistic enough not to demand full information, but does suggest that the information given should highlight the risks involved. **He clearly understands the principle of informed consent, and has offered a clear and appropriate resolution of this problem**.

Chris has **coped well with the problems** associated with the second issue. He might have been tempted to simply suggest that the study should be abandoned in the interests of the participants' health and well-being, but has resisted this **in favour of a concrete suggestion for dealing with it**. His way of dealing with this ethical issue is **appropriate**, even if it might pose some further methodological problems for the researchers.

Students' answers to Question, part (j)

(j) Explain **two** ways in which the design of this study might affect the validity of the results.

[3 marks + 3 marks]

HELENA'S ANSWER

One problem is that the participants may act differently because they know they are taking part in an experiment. For example, participants might not want to mess up the research by saying how they really feel.

(0/3)

There might have been individual differences between the two groups at the beginning of the study e.g in terms of personality, gender or even cultural differences, and this may have affected the way that they responded to stress during the study.

(2/3)

CHRIS'S ANSWER

The research might have been affected by factors that are outside of the researcher's control (e.g. the amount of other stress experienced by the participants in the week they were taking the drug). This may have interfered with the accuracy of both the heart rate and stress ratings taken during the week.

(3/3)

Both groups of participants had sought help for their stress symptoms. This meant that they were at least trying to take some sort of control over their predicament. The perception of control has been shown to decrease stress levels, and this may have influenced their 'recovery' over the course of the study.

(3/3)

How to score full marks

Part (j)

HELENA'S ANSWER

Helena appears to be confused over the normal procedures used in this research, where participants are usually unaware of their involvement in a clinical manipulation. **Helena has compounded this misunderstanding with her choice of example.** We are actually told in the stimulus material for this study that participants did not know they were part of a clinical trial of the drug. **They would not, therefore, have adjusted their behaviour in the way suggested by Helena.** Her answer therefore earns no marks.

Helena has cleverly **used her knowledge of another area of the specification to highlight the moderating effects of individual differences in the stress response.** She has fortunately given examples (personality, gender etc.), which has elaborated her response sufficiently to earn 2 of the 3 marks, but would have needed the problems posed by these differences to be stated more explicitly for the full 3 marks.

CHRIS'S ANSWER

Chris quite rightly explains that studies such as this are 'more likely to be affected by factors that are outside the researcher's control'. **He has wisely qualified this by giving an example drawn from this study** (i.e. that participants may differ in the levels of stress they experienced in the week while taking the drug). He goes on to **explain** in what way this might affect the validity of the results. Chris's answer earns him the full 3 marks.

Like Helena, Chris has **used his knowledge of physiological psychology to criticise the design of this study.** He has suggested that the perceived control implied by participants seeking help may have in some way lowered their levels of stress **without the influence of drugs.** As Chris points out, this is **supported by research evidence so is worthy of full marks.**

Don't forget ...

- **Make sure you read the question carefully** and **give no more and no less** than the question's actual requirements.

- **When asked for a description or explanation, provide some detail.** Giving examples (Chris does this a lot) may help to convince the examiner that you know what you are talking about.

- If you are asked to outline or describe **more than one** feature or explanation, **remember that each is marked independently,** so **don't spend too much time on one to the detriment of the other.**

- Unless you are merely asked to 'identify' or 'state' something (usually indicated by the award of 1 mark rather than 2 or 3), **you must write in complete sentences.** This contributes to your overall **Quality of Written Communication** (QoWC) mark.

Experiments

The **laboratory experiment** gives the experimenter greater ability to **control and alter the variables being tested**. Because of this, the experimenter can eliminate many extraneous variables that might otherwise affect the results. In the **field experiment**, participants are **not aware that they are taking part in an experiment**. This replaces the artificial setting of the laboratory with a more natural one. The **natural experiment** is not regarded as a true experiment because **the independent variable is not under the control of the experimenter** and it is not possible to exert control over the allocation of participants to conditions.

Investigations using correlational analysis

Correlational analyses yield **graphical and mathematical representations** of the degree and direction of relatedness of two sets of measurements. This can be achieved through **scattergrams** and through **correlation coefficients**. Knowledge of the degree and direction of any relationship enables us to predict (with varying degrees of certainty) a value of one variable if we know the value of the other. **Correlations can be used when experiments are inappropriate or impossible, but do not tell us anything about causality.**

Questionnaire surveys

These are techniques whereby **the investigator makes use of a structured set of questions to obtain information about a particular area**. Questions can be **fixed-choice**, where respondents can only choose from a fixed set of options, or **open-ended**, where respondents can say whatever they like. Surveys tend to be an **economical method of gathering a lot of information** from a lot of people, **but their effectiveness may be limited by poor design**, such as the use of leading or ambiguous questions.

Naturalistic observations

Naturalistic observations take place in the **natural setting in which we would normally observe a particular behaviour**. The researcher does not attempt to manipulate any aspect of the situation, but merely observes (although people may react to the presence of the observer). Such observations may yield more natural behaviour (compared to investigations in the laboratory) and may produce greater insights because of the longer period of observation. **Because the observer has no control over an independent variable, no conclusions about cause and effect are possible**.

Interviews

Interviews typically involve **face-to-face interaction between the interviewer and the interviewee**. Interviews may be **highly structured** (in terms of the questions asked) or **unstructured**. The former may involve a more objective form of interviewing, whereas the more flexible and searching unstructured interview may be a rich source of **qualitative** data. Interviewers are trained to deliver questions without bias or encouragement to interviewees to answer them in a certain way. **If interviewers cannot develop an appropriate rapport with their interviewees, then questions may not be answered in an open and honest manner**.

Questions for you to try

Question

In order to investigate possible gender differences in the aggressive behaviour of pre-school children, two psychologists are given access to a local playgroup to carry out observations of the children who attend there. After carrying out a pilot study at a different playgroup, the psychologists observed children during a one-hour free play session. They recorded any incidents of physical aggression (e.g. pushing, hitting, etc.) and verbal aggression (e.g. taunting, shouting, etc.) shown by each child towards another child. They observed a total of 10 boys and 10 girls and, for each sex, totalled the number of incidents of each type of aggression observed in the one-hour observational period. A summary of their results can be seen graphically in Figure 1.

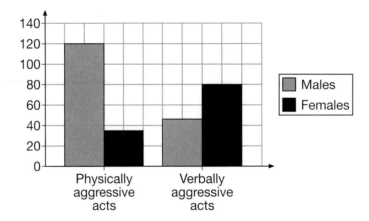

Figure 1 **Gender differences in the incidence of aggressive acts in a one-hour observation period**

(a) Suggest an appropriate non-directional (two-tailed) hypothesis for this study.
[2 marks]

(b) Why did the researchers choose both physical **and** verbal aggression in this study? [3 marks]

(c) Give one advantage of using a pilot study. [2 marks]

(d) Give one advantage and one disadvantage of the research method used in this study. [2 marks + 2 marks]

(e) What steps could the researchers take to make their observations more 'reliable'? [3 marks]

(f) Give two conclusions that might be drawn from the information in Figure 1. [2 marks + 2 marks]

(g) Describe two problems with this study that might have limited the validity of any conclusions drawn. [3 marks + 3 marks]

(h) If this study were to be repeated, explain how the researchers might have overcome each of the problems that you described in (g). [3 marks + 3 marks]

Answers are given on pp. 90–92.

Chapter 1 Memory

🎯 How to score full marks

(a) Working memory consists of several slave systems that can work independently from one another under the control of the central executive. This key component of the model acts like a planner and it co-ordinates the distribution and collection of information from its slave-systems as well as from LTM. It can handle information from any sensory modality, but its storage capacity is limited. The slave-systems have specific roles and all have restricted capacity. They can operate independently of one another so more than one task can be carried out simultaneously provided they make use of different slave-systems. The phonological loop acts like an inner voice and allows rehearsal of verbal items and has a duration of approx. 2 seconds. The visuo-spatial scratchpad acts like an inner eye and is responsible for processing visual stimuli such as a tracking task. A later addition to the model was the primary acoustic store which acts as an inner ear and can process non-verbal sounds.

> **Examiner's comment**
>
> This answer does not include irrelevant material about other models. **All the main features of the working memory model are described here and the description is accurate and detailed.** Note how the **use of succinct terms** such as 'sensory modality', 'tracking task' and 'non-verbal sounds' allows you to cut down on unnecessary words – you do not have to explain these terms to the examiner. Note also that it is not necessary to write about the effectiveness of the model. It would also be acceptable to offer an account of the Levels of Processing Model here.

(b) Conrad carried out a study into encoding in STM. He showed participants a set of capital letters on a screen and asked them to write them down in the order that they had appeared. The letters were presented very quickly, so participants had to rely on their STM to hold them for long enough to write them down. Conrad had two conditions – one condition contained a set of letters that sound similar when they are said out loud, e.g. P, V, B, D, T etc., and the other condition consisted of letters that do not sound the same, e.g. K, Z, M, X, F. Even though he only presented sets that were within the digit span (e.g. 7 letters or less), participants consistently recalled fewer letters in the acoustically similar condition than in the dissimilar condition.

> **Examiner's comment**
>
> An appropriate study has been described although there are others which are equally suitable, for example Baddeley's study on acoustic coding or the study by Kintsch and Buschke (however, in both these studies, you would need to concentrate on the findings related to **STM only**). Both procedure and findings have been **accurately described** and the candidate has included sufficient detail for full marks. Note that it is not necessary to give equal weighting to the procedures and the findings for full marks. It will often be the case that there is more to say about one aspect of a study than another. The important point is that you **address both requirements**, even if you do not write exactly the same amount for each. **Take care not to confuse conclusions with findings.** You will not lose any marks for including irrelevant information, but you will be wasting precious time. Any study of the nature of short-term memory would be acceptable here. Other possibilities would be Baddeley's study of the capacity of memory or Peterson and Peterson's study of the duration of memory. It would also be perfectly legitimate to describe a study on forgetting in STM.

(c) One reason why witnesses might be unreliable is that they reconstruct their memory for events in line with previously stored knowledge. Bartlett, in his 'War of the Ghosts' study, for example, showed that people changed the details of the original story in order to make it more consistent with their own experience. However, his research is criticized for being poorly controlled and Gauld and Stephenson found that people could recall stories accurately if they were led to believe that accuracy was very important. Foster also found that accuracy was greater for a group of participants who believed that their testimony was to be used in a genuine case than for a group who knew that they were simply taking part in an experiment. This highlights the problems of applying laboratory results to real-life situations and shows that some psychological research may underestimate people's ability to recall events accurately.

Loftus has shown in a number of studies that people can be influenced by misleading post-event information. For example, she showed participants slides depicting the events leading up to a car accident and then asked them questions in which she included some false information about the nature of a road sign. Participants fed the misleading information were later more likely to pick the wrong slide in a recognition test. She also found that the tendency to pick the wrong slide persisted even when participants were promised money as a reward for accurate recognition. This made her think that the original event had been deleted from memory and replaced by the inaccurate version. Evidence from the cognitive interview technique suggests that this is not the case. Eyewitnesses can be reliable if the correct cues are provided, which suggests that the original information is still available. It also seems that some of Loftus' methods might have given a false picture of witness fallibility. Other researchers have shown, for example, that witnesses are more accurate if they are asked to recall details in chronological order rather than in the random order required by Loftus.

Loftus herself found that there is a limit to how much witnesses can be misled by false information. She found that participants correctly recalled the colour of a stolen purse (red) even though they had been fed later information from a respectable source (a professor) that the purse was brown. So, it looks as though key elements that stand out are less likely to be distorted than things that are less central.

In one study on weapon focus, Loftus found that anxiety about the weapon detracted attention from other details such as the attacker's face etc. and so led to lower reliability. However, Christianson and Hubinette found that, in real-life situations, fear actually heightens accuracy. It seems, then, that laboratory experiments might give a false picture of the extent of eyewitness unreliability. However, it is clear that errors of recall do occur and research such as that carried out by Loftus has been important in investigating some of the reasons why and in suggesting ways to improve accuracy.

Examiner's comment

This material is **clearly focused on the question** and makes a good attempt at evaluating relevant psychological research. Although the question asks for the extent of **support** for the idea that eyewitness testimony is unreliable, it is **important to give both sides of the argument**. It does not matter which side of the argument is eventually more convincing provided that you discuss both and include research evidence to support your points. A range of studies has been used effectively to make clear evaluative points. Note that it is not necessary to include long descriptions of research studies. This will waste time and gain you few marks. Although there are 6 AO1 marks available for this answer, **you should only include as much descriptive detail as is necessary to draw an appropriate conclusion.** You have a limited time to answer this question (approx. 18 minutes) and so you will have to be selective. The example given above is only one way of tackling the question. It could have been successfully answered using different examples of research, e.g. more evidence based on schema theory or evidence from face recognition studies. The key thing is **to show your ability to select material appropriately and to use it effectively to answer the question set.**

This answer is very good because it fulfils all the criteria for the highest mark band. It provides **appropriate, carefully selected and relevant** descriptive material. The AO2 commentary is also **informed and thorough** and material has been used **very effectively** to address the question.

How to score full marks

(a) Under conditions of arousal, the pituitary gland releases adrenocorticotrophic hormone (ACTH) into the bloodstream. This travels to the adrenal cortex, which releases corticosteroids. These mobilize energy resources and maintain blood flow and heart rate to get oxygen to the muscles that may be needed in a 'fight or flight' response.

During arousal, the sympathetic division of the autonomic nervous system stimulates the adrenal medulla to release the hormones adrenaline and noradrenaline into the bloodstream. These hormones, in conjunction with corticosteroids, reinforce sympathetic arousal by stimulating heart rate and mobilizing further energy resources in the body. This enables the body to deal with the stressor by activating a 'fight or flight' response.

> **Examiner's comment**
>
> The outline of two ways in which the body responds to stress (pituitary-adrenal cortex and sympathetic-adrenal medulla activity) are **accurate and detailed. You are only asked for the ways that the body responds, so there is no need for elaborate introductions or unnecessary detail** about the nature of the stressor.

(b) Johansson et al. (1978) studied workers in a Swedish sawmill, comparing the stress levels of 'finishers' (who finished the timber as the last stage of the process) with other workers in the sawmill. They recorded workers' levels of stress hormones at various intervals during workdays and rest days, and looked at patterns of absenteeism and sickness.

They concluded that the work environment of the 'finishers' made them particularly vulnerable to stress. They were responsible for the wages of the whole factory, their job was highly skilled but monotonous and repetitive, and the job was machine paced (giving them no control over the pace of the work).

> **Examiner's comment**
>
> This answer clearly presents the **procedures and conclusions** without being distracted into describing either the aims or findings. These are both **accurate and detailed** and are also described in the same amount of detail (although this is not necessary to achieve full marks).

(c) Stress-inoculation training is a cognitive-behavioural approach to stress management. Clients are first encouraged to relive stressful situations in their own lives and consider how they had reacted to them. In the second stage they are taught strategies for coping with stressful situations, and finally they are given the opportunity to apply these in the real world, with successful coping acting as reinforcement. In hardiness training, clients are first taught how to recognise signs of stress and then to analyse the effectiveness of their current coping strategies. An essential part of hardiness training is self-improvement, as the trainer begins with challenges the client can cope with before moving on to more complex problems.

Stress inoculation is potentially a very powerful stress management technique, because it combines cognitive strategies for dealing with stress with behavioural therapy (training in new skills). Despite this, however, there is little evidence from properly controlled studies that stress inoculation is an effective method of dealing with stress. Also, the technique requires high levels of motivation and commitment from the client, so is not a quick and easy fix for stressful situations. The application of this technique may also be weakened by habits acquired over our lifetime (e.g. denial), even if these habits have been ineffective methods of stress management.

A major problem for hardiness training is that the underlying concept of hardiness itself has been criticised. Although the role of control in stress management is clear, the importance of the other two components, commitment and challenge, is less well established. Early studies supporting the effectiveness of hardiness training were restricted to a sample of white, middle-class businessmen, although more recently hardiness training has been used successfully with Olympic swimmers and with the US military. However, as with stress-inoculation, hardiness training is lengthy and requires commitment and motivation. As such it would never be a rapid solution to stress management problems.

Examiner's comments

All the information given in this answer is focused on the question set. Although the question invites you to outline and evaluate 'two or more' approaches, an answer that includes more than two might drift into a more superficial level of description and evaluation than one that is restricted to just two. The first paragraph is all description, which is a good idea because it focuses both the student and the examiner on the fact that all the necessary AO1 content is in the same place. Doing it this way means that the remaining material in the answer should be AO2. Note that no names, dates or even stage names are evident in this first paragraph. This isn't a problem, as it is the quality of the psychology that gets the marks, not memory for names and dates. Abandoning technical terms completely in your exam isn't a good idea however, as their use constitutes part of your 'quality of written communication' mark which is given for the paper as a whole.

The second and third paragraphs are entirely AO2, with important 'lead-in' phrases being used to good effect. So, instead of just being told that stress-inoculation requires motivation and commitment from the client, we are told that the consequence of this is that it is not a quick and easy fix for stressful situations. Students often use the fact that Kobasa's early research was on middle-class businessmen as a criticism of hardiness training. Merely stating this fact is not a particularly effective form of evaluation. However, adding the riposte that more recent studies have demonstrated the wider effectiveness of this technique does make this point far more effective.

This is a good answer because it fulfils all the criteria of the highest mark band. It gives an accurate and detailed exposition of relevant psychological approaches to stress management. The AO2 commentary is likewise informed and thorough and the material has been used in a highly effective manner throughout the answer. This answer would receive maximum marks.

How to score full marks

(a) One problem with this definition concerns the concept of desirability. Many people would agree that one purpose of defining abnormality is to identify behaviours which are undesirable and potentially harmful for the individual concerned, so that help can be given. If you define abnormality purely in terms of statistical infrequency, you would include things such as exceptionally high intelligence or courage or creativity. These are not thought to be undesirable and do not need treatment.

Another problem is that some types of behaviour which are seen as psychologically abnormal (e.g. depression and anxiety) are not particularly rare. For example, a recent large-scale survey found that almost half the people who responded had experienced a psychological disorder at some point in their life.

> **Examiner's comment**
>
> Two appropriate limitations of the statistical infrequency definition are given and they are clearly separated into two paragraphs. **Note that you do not have to write exactly the same amount for both, provided that you explain each one clearly.** It is useful, but not absolutely necessary, to give examples to illustrate your answer. Other limitations would have been just as acceptable, e.g. the gender and cultural issues that can affect statistical data. Note that you **do not have to waste time explaining what is meant by the term 'statistical infrequency'.**

(b) The behavioural model makes the assumption that people who exhibit abnormal behaviour do so because they have learned maladaptive patterns. Behaviourists do not use the term 'mental disorder' or 'mental illness' because they are only interested in behaviour and do not concern themselves with internal mental structures. They believe that maladaptive patterns of behaviour are acquired and maintained through the processes of classical and operant conditioning and social learning, i.e. through imitation and vicarious reinforcement. For example, someone could acquire a phobia about heights by associating the nausea and dizziness experienced by looking down from a great height with the height itself (classical conditioning). The individual would then avoid heights and be rewarded by no longer experiencing the unpleasant sensations (operant conditioning).

> **Examiner's comment**
>
> An appropriate model has been chosen (behavioural) and the assumptions are clearly outlined. It can often be useful to give an example because this demonstrates to the examiner that you understand the issues involved. You are not being asked to evaluate the model here so there is no need to waste time in considering the strengths and weaknesses of the approach. Similarly, you would be wasting time if you used other models as a point of comparison. Note how the use of specialist terms such as 'classical conditioning', 'operant conditioning' and 'vicarious reinforcement' allows you to express ideas succinctly. Other acceptable choices for this question include the psychodynamic, medical and cognitive models.

(c) According to the behavioural model, eating disorders arise from a combination of classical and operant conditioning or through modelling. This view is supported by cross-cultural studies which suggest that eating disorders occur more in societies where slimness is valued e.g. in Western societies. Even within Western culture, Garner has found that ballet dancers, for whom slimness is essential, are more prone to develop anorexia than other girls. However, cross-cultural studies can be difficult to interpret and the low rates of eating disorders may reflect a reluctance to report such problems rather than a difference in attitudes to body size. It is also difficult for the behavioural model to account for the fact that dieting continues to the point of dangerously low body weight, although behaviourists might explain this in terms of the attention (positive reinforcement) they receive.

Fairburn et al., found that people with both anorexia and bulimia were more perfectionist and more negative in their self-evaluation than control groups. This supports the cognitive explanation of distorted thinking patterns. However, this model does not explain where the distorted ideas come from in the first place. It may be that they are an effect rather than a cause of eating disorders.

The psychodynamic model offers several explanations mainly related to experiences in childhood. McClelland et al found that 30% of clients attending an eating disorder clinic had a history of childhood sexual abuse. They suggested that such traumatic experiences are repressed at the time and emerge later as eating disorders. However, not everyone with an eating disorder has experienced sexual abuse and people who have been sexually abused do not necessarily develop eating disorders. Bruch believed that eating disorders are linked to sexual immaturity. One suggestion is that girls associate fatness with pregnancy and so avoid eating in order to avoid pregnancy. This is a less convincing explanation for bulimia and, in any case, does not account for anorexia in boys.

Since no single psychological explanation seems to be adequate, it might be that biological factors play a part. Using twin studies, Holland found evidence for genetic transmission. Ward, however, found that environmental factors were better predictors of eating disorders than genetic. Other biological explanations include malfunction of the hypothalamus or of certain neurotransmitters e.g. serotonin, but there is little conclusive evidence. The main problem with biochemical research is that it is difficult to disentangle cause from effect.

Eating disorders are complex and it seems likely that both biological and psychological factors contribute to their origins and maintenance.

Examiner's comment

This material is **focused on the question from the outset and includes reference to various psychological explanations for eating disorders.** The question requires you to put forward the case for psychological explanations of eating disorders, but it is helpful as part of your evaluation to contrast such explanations with those arising from the biological model. **You do not have much time to write your answer so do not spend it on lengthy descriptions of the various explanations,** although you can gain up to 6 marks for AO1 material. The focus should be on assessing the **adequacy** of such explanations and you can do this by providing evidence for and against them.

Do not worry too much about remembering the dates of studies that you use to provide empirical support for your arguments, but it is useful to try to remember the names of the researchers. This makes it easier for the examiners to recognise the study. Because of time restraints, you will have to be **selective** in the number and nature of the evaluative points you make. There are many other studies and/or examples that you could have used effectively in this answer – the choice is up to you **provided that the points are all relevant and meet the requirements of the question.** It is important to remember that the question refers to 'eating disorders' and not simply to anorexia nervosa. You might find that you know more about possible causal explanations for anorexia, but make sure that you include some references to bulimia as well.

Remember that there are two marks on each paper for the quality of written communication. It is worthwhile trying to write clearly and accurately and to use specialist terms correctly.

🎯 How to score full marks

(a) *Social influence* is the way in which another person or group of people may affect the attitudes or behaviours of an individual.

Minority influence refers to the effect of a persuasive smaller group or individual (minority) changing the attitudes or behaviours of a larger group (majority).

Obedience is complying with a direct instruction. It usually happens when one person thinks another has the right to give orders.

> **Examiner's comment**
>
> **All three terms are clearly explained.** You do not have to provide exactly the same length of answer for each as long as you have given a clear explanation.

(b) One reason why people may yield to minority influence is that they notice a consistent message being delivered by the minority. For example, members of a consistent minority will not contradict each other (i.e. they show inter-individual consistency). Individual members of the minority will also be consistent over time (i.e. they show intra-individual consistency). Such consistency makes minorities appear genuine and worth listening to. Thus they are noticed and majorities pay them more attention.

Another reason why people yield to minorities is that they see them as showing commitment, i.e. as willing to make sacrifices if necessary. For example, members of the civil rights movement in the US and the suffragette movement in the UK were willing to go to prison. Gradually, respect for the minority views grows and the majority is converted.

> **Examiner's comment**
>
> **Two relevant ways** in which minorities exert their influence are outlined. Other ways are by showing flexibility and being in line with social trends. Make it clear when you move from outlining one point to outlining another.

(c) Ethical issues are the concerns that psychologists have about what is right or acceptable in the way they carry out their research, e.g. whether or not it is ever acceptable to deceive participants about the true nature of an experiment. The use of deception, insufficient informed consent and failure to safeguard participants, perhaps causing them long-term psychological harm, are some of the ethical objections levelled against research in the area of social influence.

Milgram certainly deceived his participants about the true nature of his research, but he claimed this was necessary if obedience was to be researched properly. His critics argue that other methods, such as participants role-playing the situation, could be used instead. Others disagree, stating that the only way to find out the truth about how people behave in obedience situations is to place them in a real situation where obedience is asked of them, not by asking them to pretend! If this is so, then you cannot fully inform participants of the true nature of the study first.

Both Milgram and Zimbardo are accused of causing lasting harm to their participants by causing them to face unpleasant truths about themselves (e.g. that they were capable of giving 450 volts to someone). Zimbardo's prison simulation study was called off after only six days because those acting as guards were over zealous and some prisoners were very distressed.

Milgram answered that he did not expect to find such high levels of obedience, especially since a preliminary survey showed that few people thought anyone normal would give high levels of shocks. Therefore, he could not have predicted the discomfort that many of the participants experienced. Nevertheless, he did carry on repeating his procedures many times with variations. But, by doing this, he found out what aspects of situations caused people to obey most readily. These are important discoveries.

Both Milgram and Zimbardo have responded to their critics by claiming that their thorough debriefing processes ensured that the participants left the laboratory feeling OK about themselves. During debriefing the purpose of the study and the reason for the deception were explained. Others, however, argue that debriefing cannot justify unethical aspects of an investigation. Milgram also sent questionnaires to his participants and had some of them psychologically assessed. None reported any long-term ill effects, but maybe they still saw themselves as part of a study and influenced by demand characteristics.

Psychologists today are still divided as to whether the ethical objections to social influence research are valid or not. Some (e.g. Baumrind) believe that it is wrong to deceive people or to take any risks with their well-being. Others think that the importance of the topics being studied justified the slight risk posed to those who participated. Zimbardo proposes more (but better supervised) research be carried out to investigate these issues.

Examiner's comment

All the information given in this answer is focused on the question set. The term 'ethical issues' is explained and three important ethical objections are identified at the start (AO1 content). Each is then discussed with reference to Milgram's and/or Zimbardo's research with arguments on both sides of the debate offered (AO2 content). The answer concludes by giving two current views about the ethics of social influence research. Because of time constraints, it is inevitable that only a limited amount of material can be covered. This is OK but you need to **select relevant points that enable you to show your understanding of the material and your evaluative skills to best effect**. Remember that 2 marks are allocated for the quality of written communication shown in a paper. It is worthwhile, therefore, trying to write clearly and accurately, using specialist terms correctly.

🎯 How to score full marks

(a) There is no gender difference in the incidence of aggressive behaviours in male and female pre-school children.

> **Examiner's comments**
>
> The essential characteristic of a null hypothesis is that is **assumes no difference** between the populations from which the sample were taken (in this case it was pre-school male and female children). This is in contrast to any prediction made in the **alternative hypothesis**. The null hypothesis above states that there is no difference and explicitly mentions the variables being investigated. It doesn't matter that it makes no distinction between physical and verbal aggression - this might be explored in a different hypothesis.

(b) The researchers would have chosen to observe both physical and verbal aggression to take account of possible gender differences in the *type* of aggressive behaviour shown by the different sexes. It is possible, for example, that the more obvious physical aggression is a characteristic of male aggression, whilst the less obvious verbal aggression is found more often in females.

> **Examiner's comments**
>
> Although it is still a matter of debate whether these gender differences in the **type of aggression are more real than imagined, this does seem a good reason for** documenting both in this investigation. **This answer explains this reason clearly, and is sufficiently elaborated to ensure the full 3 marks available.**

(c) An advantage of a pilot study is that it enables a researcher to carry out a 'dry run' of all procedures so that any problems can be discovered and dealt with prior to the study proper.

> **Examiner's comments**
>
> This simple statement demonstrates one of the main advantages of doing a pilot study. It is sufficiently detailed to deserve both of the marks available. Note that this question doesn't add the words 'in this study', so it is all right to answer the question without referring to this particular study. **You do need to look carefully at questions to see if they need to be answered 'in context' or, as here, in more general terms.**

(d) The main advantage of naturalistic observation is that it enables researchers to explore behaviour in its natural setting without the artificiality of a laboratory. This means that they can be more confident that the behaviour being observed (e.g. aggressive behaviour) is also more likely to be natural.

The main disadvantage of this method is that because there is no control over an independent variable, it is not possible to form conclusions about cause-effect relationships. In this study it would not be possible to conclude that the differences in aggressive behaviour were a product of gender differences.

> **Examiner's comments**
>
> This is a clear and accurate statement of the most obvious advantage of this method of research. It is always a good idea (if it is not named in the question) to **identify** the method in your answer, just in case the examiner is struggling to decide what method you are actually evaluating. Although the question does not specifically ask **why** naturalistic observation was used in **this** study, it is also wise to draw any necessary illustrative examples from the present study. The disadvantage is also clear, accurate and detailed. Although the first sentence

would probably be enough to capture the full two marks, if time allows, it is a good idea to illustrate your answer by showing in real terms how that disadvantage would limit **this** study.

(e) In order to make observations more reliable it would be necessary to carefully operationalise physical and verbal aggression. These categories of behaviour can then form the basis of a structured observation sheet. This could be tested and adjusted during the pilot study. After the observations, the ratings of each observer could be compared to establish the degree of inter-observer reliability.

> **Examiner's comments**
>
> **It pays to read every question very carefully.** This one asks how the researchers might make their observations more reliable. It doesn't ask what reliability is or how it might be checked. Don't always assume that the same answer will suffice regardless of the particular spin in the question. **This is a comprehensive account** (given the time available) of four steps towards greater reliability (operationalise, structure, pilot study, compare) and would be worth maximum marks.

(f) It appears that males show a greater incidence of total aggressive acts compared to females, therefore we may conclude that male pre-school children behave more aggressively during free play. It is also evident that there is a difference in the **type** of aggressive behaviour shown by male and female pre-school children. Males depend more on physical aggression, and females on verbal aggression

> **Examiner's comments**
>
> These two conclusions both follow from the information given in Figure 1. Although there is no numerical data available, it is fairly obvious from Figure 1 that male aggression is more evident than female aggression, but that there are clear differences in the type, with females actually showing **more** verbal aggression than males. **There is certainly enough in this answer to be worth full marks for both conclusions.**

(g) It is possible that the males and females differed in age, as the study makes no reference to the age of the children being observed. As pre-school playgroups usually take children between the ages of 3 and 5, it may be the case that the results reflect more the age make-up of the two gender groups than any gender related characteristics.

Some of the behaviours observed may have been caused by the children reacting to the presence of the observers. This may have been more evident in males than females, reflecting more a gender difference in the need to show off than in aggressive behaviour.

> **Examiner's comments**
>
> The two problems given are appropriate and clearly explained. Notice that in each of these, the first sentence **identifies the problem,** and the next sentence **elaborates this** by explaining why this would have limited the validity of any conclusions that might be drawn. Remember that in questions such as this (where there are 3 marks available), the examiner must be able to discriminate between answers that are worth 3, 2 and 1 mark. You should elaborate your answer sufficiently within the time available to make sure that you access the full 3 marks available.

(h) The observations could be repeated, but this time the observers would note the age of each child being observed. Graphs could then be drawn to demonstrate any interaction of age and gender. It may be necessary to include other playgroups to increase the number of children in each age category.

Observers might spend more time at the playgroup prior to the study so that children grew used to them and no longer reacted to their presence in the same way. Alternatively, they might have used more covert observational methods such as using a hidden video camera to record the children at play.

> **Examiner's comments**
>
> These are sensible resolutions of the problem. As mentioned in the previous answer, there **may** be age effects on aggressive behaviour, and the solution suggested is sufficiently straightforward and clearly detailed. **Again, note the use of elaboration to ensure the full 3 marks available for this part of the answer.** The second problem can also be dealt with fairly easily. Rather than simply saying 'use a video camera', this answer details **why** reactivity must be dealt with and then offers two alternatives for eliminating its effects. As before, this answer is accurate and sufficiently elaborated for full marks.

C Collins · *do brilliantly!*

InstantRevision

AS Psychology

The ideal **solution** to **last-minute** revision

AS Instant Revision Psychology   ISBN 0 00 721558 4

Ideal for last-minute revision, this handy pocket-size book covers all the essential facts and includes 'Check yourself' questions to ensure you have all the knowledge at your fingertips.

Contents

Also available from Collins:

Do Brilliantly at A2 Psychology   ISBN 0 00 717178 1

This follow-up to Exam Practice at AS Psychology gives you all the help and advice you need to do brilliantly at A2, including guidance with synoptic questions.

Contents

Social Psychology

Physiological Psychology

Cognitive Psychology

Developmental Psychology

Comparative Psychology

Perspectives: Individual Differences

Perspectives: Issues

Perspectives: Debates

Perspectives: Approaches

Other titles in the series: